Sailing for
BEGINNERS

Sailing for BEGINNERS

Jeff Toghill

Arco Publishing Company, Inc.
New York

Published by Arco Publishing Company, Inc. 219 Park Avenue South, New York, N.Y. 10003

Copyright © 1976 by Jeff Toghill

Printed in Great Britain
First published in Australia by A. H. & A. W. Reed Pty. Ltd.
This edition published in Great Britain by Ward Lock Ltd., member of the Pentos Group.

Library of Congress Cataloging in Publication Data

Toghill, Jeff E
    Sailing for beginners.

    1. Sailing. I. Title.
GV811.T56 1977   797.1'24   76-30640
ISBN 0-668-04223-0
ISBN 0-688-04220-6 pbk.

Contents

Chapter 1   The Boat

The types and classes of dinghies and small boats are too numerous to list in this chapter. Apart from the hundreds of international classes which are common to all countries, almost every harbour, bay, lake or waterway has its own special class adapted to the conditions which exist in that part of the world.

Equally lengthy would be a detailed list of classes of yachts and larger vessels, to say nothing, of course, of the hundreds of boats which do not fall into the category of a class boat. However, all boats, no matter what size or class, can be classified under one *rig* or another, and the following illustrations show the different rigs as applied to the larger yachts.

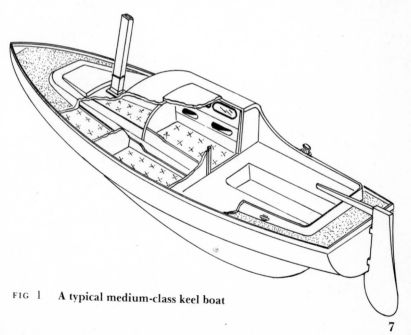

FIG 1   **A typical medium-class keel boat**

THE SLOOP

Most common of all rigs and gaining in popularity every year, the sloop is the simplest form of rig, having only one headsail and one mainsail. The jib can be changed to a larger or smaller size, giving greater or lesser sail area as required. It requires the minimum amount of rigging and the minimum number of crew.

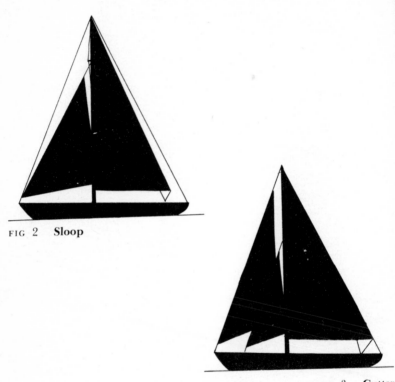

FIG 2 **Sloop**

FIG 3 **Cutter**

THE CUTTER

This rig was popular in earlier years but is now going out of vogue. It varies from the sloop rig only in that it carries two headsails instead of one. These are the jib and staysail which, of course, require extra crew to handle the additional sheets.

8

Timber built cutter

THE KETCH

Most popular of the two-masted rigs, the ketch rig comprises headsails, main and mizzen. The mizzen is usually fairly large and the mizzen mast is stepped well inboard from the stern, *forward* of the steering position. The rig may carry one or two headsails; with one it is referred to as a *Sloop-rigged Ketch,* with two as a *Cutter-rigged Ketch.* Off the wind a *Mizzen Staysail* may be set between the masts.

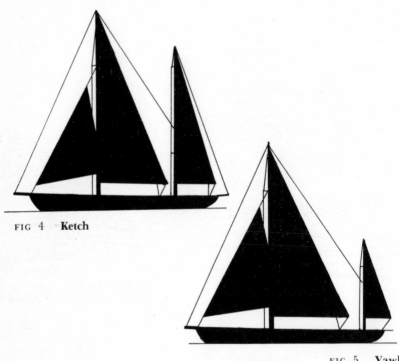

FIG 4 **Ketch**

FIG 5 **Yawl**

THE YAWL

This rig differs from the ketch rig only in the size and location of the mizzen. In a yawl rig the mizzen is much smaller and the mizzen mast usually located well aft, *astern* of the sailing position. As with ketch rig, yawl rig may have one or two headsails and may also carry the mizzen staysail.

10

THE SCHOONER

Most graceful of all rigs, the schooner rig is slowly disappearing from the yachting scene. It comprises two masts, the foremast being shorter than the main. There are a number of different sail plans that can be carried with a schooner rig, the most popular being the rig illustrated. Schooners invariably carry more than one headsail and in the divided rig illustrated above carry two sails between the masts. The lower is the *staysail* and the upper the *fisherman staysail*.

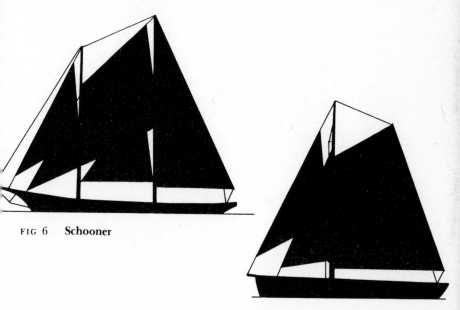

FIG 6 **Schooner**

FIG 7 **Gaff rig**

GAFF RIG

Although rare today, the gaff rig enjoyed much popularity in early yachting years. Its main disadvantage lies in the gaff itself—a heavy, cumbersome boom which carries the head of the mainsail. In the old days sails were larger, and the gaff gave more opportunity for carrying large sails, as the gaff rigged sail has four corners as opposed to the three on modern bermuda rig sails. Gaff rig makes a boat very fast off the wind, but heavy and less easy to handle on the wind.

11

The Sails

Most modern sails are made from synthetic materials such as dacron or terylene. These materials are almost rot-proof and impervious to the effects of wind and weather. The canvas sails—more common in the years gone by, although there are still quite a number in use today—had to be washed in fresh water and thoroughly dried after use to prevent mould or rot attacking them.

Sails are cut and sewn to shape in a sailmaker's loft. Thus sails are said to be "lofted" when they are manufactured. A sail is never flat. A good sailmaker will cut considerable *shape* into a sail, i.e., he will so form the shape of the sail that in cross section, it will appear something like the aerofoil section of an aeroplane wing. It is this shaping of a sail that decides how well it will drive a boat. For strong winds the sail will have a flatter shape, for lighter winds a deeper curve or "belly" to enable it to gather up the lighter winds.

Another important factor in sail-making is the weight of the cloth used. It is measured in ounces per square yard. Thus a heavy, strong cloth used for heavy-weather sails will be many ounces heavier per square foot than the light, gossamer-type material used for light weather spinnakers.

In a racing yacht it is not unusual to have a *wardrobe* of up to twenty sails. These are made up as follows:

For normal weather—
   One medium weight mainsail
   Two or three medium weight jibs
   Two medium weight spinnakers
For light weather—
   Two lightweight mainsails
   Two lightweight jibs
   Two lightweight Genoas
   One lightweight ghoster or drifter
   Two lightweight spinnakers
For heavy weather—
   One storm jib
   One storm main
   Two heavy duty spinnakers

There are, of course, numerous other sails, many of which are cut to the individual design of the yachtsman or the designer. But, basically, the wardrobe described above would be that of a well fitted-out ocean racer.

Smaller boats, of course, require smaller sails, some of the very small dinghies using only one sail. Depending on their design, catamarans also frequently have only one sail.

The size and shape of a sail are usually decided by the designer. He takes into account the shape of the hull, the boat's speed through the water, and the type of sailing she will do before designing the most suitable sail.

One of the common fallacies about sailing is that the more sail area the faster the boat will be. This is quite untrue and sails are in fact becoming smaller and smaller, yet the boats are moving faster. This is seen also in the design of modern aircraft wings. In the old days of Orville Wright the clumsy, slow old aircraft had an enormous wingspan. Compare this to the sleek, almost nonexistent wingspan of a supersonic jet fighter.

Most of the power derived from a suit of sails comes from the jib, and nowadays more and more designers are building boats with small mainsails and large jibs. A light weather Genoa, or large jib, is often larger than the mainsail itself—which is a complete reversal of old sailing ship design.

When a sail is delivered to the boat it is folded carefully and packed in a sailbag. It is good practice to fold the sail each time it is used, as indiscriminate folding will crease the sail and eventually cause it to lose some of its shape. As mentioned earlier the shape of the sail is all important. Fig. 8 illustrates the basic parts of a yacht's sails.

The sail has three corners: The *peak*, the *tack* and the *clew*. The peak goes to the top of the mast (or to the top of the hoist, in the case of a jib); the clew is the after corner, and the tack the forward corner. There are a number of different ways of fastening the sails to the spars and rigging, but the most common method is to use *hanks* (a kind of spring clip), for clipping on to stays, and metal or nylon *slides*, or a grooved *luff-rope* for attaching the sail to mast and boom.

Modern fibreglass trailer-sailer

The leading edge of a sail—the *luff*—is strengthened either with rope or tape, as this is where the greatest strain comes when the sail is set. One of the secrets of setting a sail is to ensure that the luff is absolutely bar-tight. Any slackness at all not only looks bad, but interferes with the performance of the boat.

For this reason, big yachts have winches at the foot of the mast to tighten up the hoisting wire (known as the *halyard*), and stretch the luff of the sail taut. Small boats rely on a small block and tackle to get their sails well set, and dinghies sometimes depend purely on good old elbow grease. But whatever the method, the luff of the sail must be really drawn tight.

The *tack* is usually just shackled down to the deck (in the case of the jib) or to the boom (in the case of the mainsail).

The *foot* of the main is also stretched, but this is not quite so important as the luff. Usually a small piece of cord is all that is needed to stretch it along the boom. In the case of the jib, the *sheets,* which are attached to the clew, stretch the foot of the sail when they are brought into use.

The *Leach,* or after end of the sail, tends sometimes to flap when it is in use. This is particularly so with the mainsail. To prevent this, pockets are sewn in the sail into which bamboo or fibreglass *battens* can be inserted to keep the leach stiff. These should always be taken out when the sail is stowed away.

Spinnakers are a different sail altogether to either the jib or main. They are *free flying* sails, which means they are not attached to any stay or to the mast, but simply held by each of the three corners. They are very full cut sails,

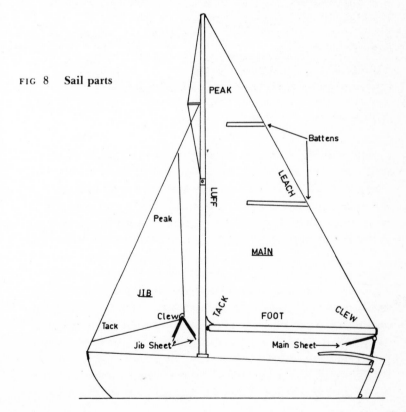

FIG 8   **Sail parts**

15

and belly out when filled with wind. For this reason they can only be carried when the wind is behind or almost behind the boat. When the wind is ahead, they collapse into a useless heap.

Although there are spinnakers for all kinds of weather, they are mostly used in moderate to light weather, as in strong winds they tend quickly to become unmanageable. Since they have a very large sail area they are very powerful and when out of control can cause much damage. There are no battens in the spinnaker.

Because of its fullness, the spinnaker tends to collapse very easily, and some support is necessary since it is not attached to a stay or the mast. The *spinnaker pole* is used to support one corner and hold it out into the wind. This gives it a chance to fill.

A full chapter (chapter 5) is devoted to the handling of spinnakers.

Standing Rigging

The standing rigging of a yacht or dinghy is almost invariably of strong wire rope, not flexible as with running rigging, and much thicker. Some yachts have rigging made out of solid rod, but this is rare except in very expensive class yachts.

The wire rope may be of galvanised plough steel or of stainless steel. There are advantages and disadvantages in both. Plough steel wire has less strength than stainless and is therefore much thicker and heavier. In racing yachts the wind resistance of standing rigging is quite considerable and thus the stainless rigging is favoured because it is lighter and thinner.

On the other hand, stainless steel wire is much more expensive than galvanised plough, and where weight and drag are of little importance the saving in cost is considerable. Stainless steel rope also tends to become brittle with age, and may snap without warning, whereas the galvanised plough wire becomes "whiskery" as it gets older, that is, small pieces of wire break off and stick out of the main body, giving warning that the rigging is due for change.

16

Fig. 9 illustrates the normal arrangement of standing rigging on a yacht.

Standing rigging is *set up* by attaching each *stay* or *shroud* to the mast and then tightening it by connecting it to *turnbuckles* or *bottle-screws* on the deck. These have the effect of pulling the wire rope tighter as they are turning, thus enabling the rigging to be tightened or slackened as desired. The *stays* are the fore and aft rigging, while the *shrouds* come down to the side of the boat. To spread the strain of the rigging evenly across a section of the hull, *chain plates* are set into the skin, often running right down to the keel, and it is to these that the turnbuckles are shackled.

Setting up, or *tuning* a mast is a very specialised business and—except for small dinghies—should not be attempted by the inexperienced. The most likely result of an improperly tuned mast is that it will be driven through the bottom of the boat!

Different parts of standing rigging may be found on a vessel, according to her design. A yacht with a *bowsprit*

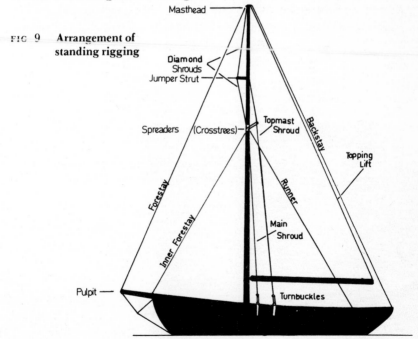

FIG 9   **Arrangement of standing rigging**

Masthead

Diamond Shrouds
Jumper Strut

Spreaders   (Crosstrees)

Topmast Shroud

Backstay

Topping Lift

Forestay

Inner Forestay

Runner

Main Shroud

Pulpit

Turnbuckles

will have a *bobstay* beneath it to prevent the bowsprit from being pulled upwards when the mast is tuned. Similarly the *bumkin* on the stern has a bobstay to hold it in position.

When a vessel has a very high mast, the rigging is not always brought entirely down to the deck. Some shrouds are rigged to run from the top of the mast to a point about halfway down. These are known as *diamond shrouds*. If there are two masts they may have a joining stay at the top, known as the *triatic stay*. Be careful not to confuse the triatic stay with the ship's radio aerial, which may also be strung between the masts.

Running Rigging

The term running rigging is given to the ropes (cotton, nylon or manila) used for controlling the sails. Although in many instances wire rope is also used for running rigging it is of a soft, flexible kind, rather than the rigid variety used for other rigging.

A sail is hoisted by means of a *halyard* which is usually a wire rope with a rope tail that runs through a pulley on the top of the mast, or at the point where the sail is

**Complicated running rigging
on a scow-type boat**

to be hoisted. Wire rope is commonly used for reasons already mentioned—the need to tighten up the luff properly when setting the sail. If the wire is wound round a winch drum, maximum power can be applied to tightening the luff.

The jib halyard is usually kept on one side of the mast and the main halyard on the other, although the halyard blocks are of course always set in the very centre of the mast. Since there is no standardisation of halyards, one of the first things to look for when setting sails on board a strange boat is which halyard is which.

The jib halyard may not run right to the top of the mast; many set only halfway up. The main, however (except in the case of a Gaff rig) sets right at the very top. For this reason it is necessary to be careful that the halyard is not allowed to run to the top of the mast, or there will be a long climb to bring it down again.

The other ropes used in running rigging are the *sheets*. These are the ropes which control the sail once it is set. The halyard is used to hoist the sail, the sheet to control it.

Because each sail is controlled independently of the other, a yacht crew usually has two *sheet hands*, one to control the jib sheet and another to control the main sheet. In the case of small dinghies, the helmsman usually controls the main sheet, leaving the jib sheet to his forward hand.

The jib sheet is attached to the sail at the clew, and is in two sections, with a sheet running down each side of the boat. When the boat *goes about* and the sail is changed from one side to the other, a sheet will be available on the other side without having to take the original sheet around the mast and down the other side. Thus only one of the two jib sheets is in use at any time.

The main sheet is usually attached to the stern end of the boom with the aid of a block and tackle, providing easier purchase for the main sheet hand. The sheet itself may be led forward through another block for convenience of handling.

Two terms are in general use for sheet handling:
'On sheets'—pull them in, pull the sails on harder.
'Ease sheets'—slack them away, ease the sails out.

19

Other terms, such as 'Off sheets', or 'Let fly' are used when the sheet is to be released altogether.

When the sails are full there is a considerable strain on the sheets; more, usually, than one can hold by hand. In larger vessels *winches* are provided to assist in handling the sheets, but in small boats and dinghies, *jam-cleats* are used. These seize the sheet when it is pulled on and hold the weight until it is flicked out of the jam-cleat to run free.

On larger boats there has to be some means of supporting the boom when the sail is not set. Usually a *crutch* is fitted under the boom at the rear of the cockpit, but as this only holds the boom when lowered, a *topping-lift* similar to that of the spinnaker pole, is fitted. This is a light wire running from the mast or some other convenient point which can be used to lift the boom up and down.

Although the gaff mentioned earlier is gradually disappearing, it is worth a small mention here. The gaff is a second boom which is hoisted up the mast in order to give the sail a four cornered shape instead of three. Additional running rigging is required, as two extra halyards must be provided to hoist the *throat* (the mast end of the gaff) and the *peak* (the outer end). The gaff is hoisted horizontally by placing even strain on both throat and peak halyards, and when the throat has reached its highest point (some way down from the top of the mast), it is made fast and the peak hoisted further. This brings the peak of the sail to a point where it is actually higher than the mast itself.

Chapter 2 **Getting Under Way**

The rigging of a boat varies considerably according to her size. As mentioned in chapter 1, the setting up and rigging of a large keel boat is a job for an expert, and should be done either by a rigger or by a shipwright. The majority of smaller craft, however, have collapsible rigging for convenience of stowage, which does not require any expert knowledge to set it up.

Boats vary again, of course, according to their class, but broadly speaking, rigging a dinghy can be summarised as follows:

1. Lay the mast along the boat with the foot near the mast step, and the masthead hanging out over the stern.

2. Attach the forestay, shrouds and other necessary rigging to the masthead, stretching them down along each side of the boat.

3. Attach the running rigging (i.e., halyards) to their position at the masthead and lay along the mast.

4. Shackle the shrouds to the chain plates on both sides.

5. Step the mast and pull it upright into position by pulling on the forestay. The shrouds will prevent it from slipping sideways once it reaches the upright position.

6. Shackle on the forestay. This may need a considerable amount of pressure, and a turnbuckle, lacing, or some other form of tightening mechanism may be necessary.

7. Sort out the various halyards and have them ready for bending on the sails. Where trapeze wires are used, these will also need to be sorted.

Bending on Sails

The procedure here is fairly similar no matter what size the vessel. In the case of dinghies and small boats, the sails

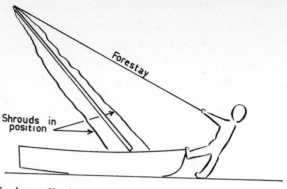

FIG 10 **Rigging a dinghy**

can be bent on while the boat is sitting on the beach, with other boats it should be done before leaving the morring.

Dinghies

1. When the mast has been rigged, turn the bow of the boat into the wind. Fit battens into the sail.

2. Attach the main halyard to the peak of the sail and thread the luff rope at the peak into the mast groove while hoisting on the halyard. (In the case of a gaff the sail must be first threaded into the gaff, and then the halyard attached to the gaff itself).

3. Repeat the procedure threading the foot of the sail into the groove along the boom.

4. When both are threaded, shackle the tack of the sail either onto the gooseneck, or the shackle provided nearby. Stretch the foot of the sail along the boom as tightly as possible by drawing on the lacing at the clew.

5. Stretch the luff of the sail as taut as possible by tightening the halyard. Make fast.

6. Shackle the main sheet, boom vang, etc.

7. Clip on the jib by means of hanks (if any) and attach it to the bow (at the tack) and halyard (at the peak). Hoist the sail and stretch it as tightly as possible by weighing down on the halyard. Make fast. Attach the sheets to the clew.

Note the importance in both cases of stretching the luff

of the sail as tightly as possible. The secret of a well set
sail is the tautness of its luff.

8. Prepare the boat for sailing by inflating buoyancy
tanks, fitting the rudder, lashing the baler, etc. During this
time, and at all times when the boat is not actually sailing
KEEP ALL SHEETS FREE. This enables the sails to flap
and the boat to remain upright. The halyards are made
secure, but never the sheets.

N.B. One of the most useful items a dinghy sailor can
fit into his boat is a paddle. It may save many a long
frustrating drift home when the wind dies. Similarly, when
the boat does not have a self-draining cockpit, a baler is
an essential item.

**Sheets free, centreboard raised.
All set to shove off**

Keel Boats

As already mentioned, the preparation of a keel boat for sailing should be undertaken while the yacht is still attached to the mooring. However, sometimes the actual hoisting of the sails is done after leaving the mooring, depending on whether or not the skipper prefers to sail off, or motor off. This again depends on location. For the purposes of this volume, it would be unwise for a beginner to sail his

Preparation is vital before getting under way

boat off the mooring unless it was in a very isolated position and there was plenty of manoeuvring room. A sudden gust of wind when the boat has just cast off the mooring and has not gathered sufficient way can be disastrous in a crowded mooring. A brief description of sailing off the mooring will be given later in this book (chapter 6).

To prepare a large yacht for sailing, then, the procedure is as follows:

1. Place the battens in the sails. Sort out the jib and main halyards, which are usually found one on either side of the mast. The wire section is the part which is attached to the sail, and although there are a number of different methods of attaching the sail to the halyard, a shackle is by far the most common.

2. Attach the peak of the mainsail to the main halyard and thread the luff rope into the mast groove, hoisting on the halyard at the same time.

3. Repeat the process, threading the foot of the sail along the boom. Stretch the sail along the boom by shackling the tack onto the gooseneck and stretching the sail with the lacing at the clew. Do not stretch the luff of the sail yet.

4. At this point the main should be lowered again and lightly lashed around the boom unless the boat is to be sailed off the mooring.

5. Clip on the jib to the forestay, by means of the hanks. Attach the peak to the jib halyard, and the tack to a shackle on the bow. Do not hoist the jib.

6. Shackle on the jib sheets or, if they are permanently attached, pass them aft through the sheeting blocks on either side into the cockpit.

7. At this point the mooring should be cast off and the boat taken out through the moorings under power. While so doing, all sheets should be freed, and the weight of the boom taken on the topping lift so that the crutch may be unshipped.

8. Once in clear water, round the boat up into the wind and hoist both sails, setting the main first. As with smaller boats, the secret of a well-set sail lies in the tautness of

its luff. Some larger vessels have winches at the foot of the mast and the halyards can be tightened up on these. Other boats have small purchases to get the extra stretch into the sail. Whatever the means, the sail must be as tight as can possibly be managed.

9. With both sails in position and the halyards secured, the engine may be shut off and sailing commenced.

It is essential that *the boat is pointing into the wind and the sheets are free* when the main is hoisted. This is because of the pressure exerted by the wind on the sail when it is drawing. If the sail fills with wind when it is halfway up it will jam or might get torn on the spreaders. When the boat is pointed into the wind the sail lies fore and aft and flaps in the wind with no pressure in it at all.

Although the descriptions given here deal only with sails fitted with luff ropes, many sails have brass or nylon tracks instead. The procedure in these cases is exactly the same, although the need to ensure that the boat is pointing into the wind is all the greater, as tracks are more liable to jam if the sail fills with wind.

Sailing a Dinghy off the Beach

Dinghies are usually launched from the beach or from a ramp. At the time of launching the boat must be fully rigged and ready to sail. The crew must be alert and ready from the moment they step on board as there is no other means of power available other than wind, and the boat has to be sailed from the moment her keel is afloat.

Unfortunately, beaches cannot be moved around to suit the sailor, and he must, therefore, be prepared to sail off whether the wind is onshore, offshore, or across the beach. The following procedures should be adopted in each case.

Onshore Breeze

This is the most difficult condition of all, as the boat has to be sailed directly into the wind, which requires the centreboard to be fully down. But the water is shallow close into the beach and it is often impossible to put the blade down much at all.

Sheets need constant trimming

1. Walk the boat into the water until she is afloat. Free all sheets and hold her head to wind, with her bow pointing seaward and sails flapping. Once the crew is aboard the skipper (who is holding the boat in position), runs her forward, gives a hard push, and jumps into the boat over the stern.

2. Bring on the sheets, both jib and main, and lower the centreboard as much as possible without touching bottom. If the breeze is very strong the sheets may be brought only half on until the centreboard can be fully lowered.

3. As the boat's head pays off, the centreboard may be lowered further. This is the crucial point and quick crew work is required to ensure that the boat takes the wind and begins sailing forward before the wind blows her back into shallow water and the centreboard has to be pulled up again.

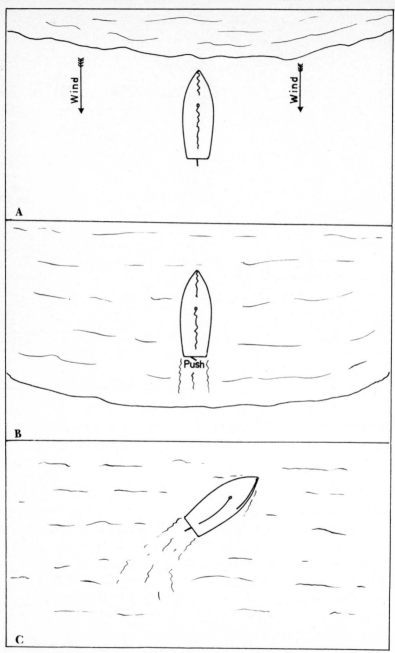

FIG 11 Sailing a dinghy off the beach—
onshore breeze

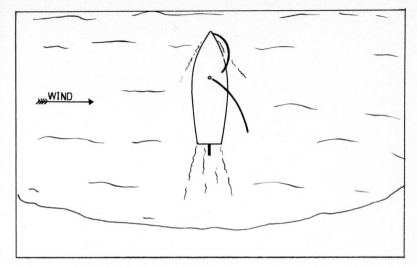

FIG 12 **Sailing a dinghy off the beach—
cross wind**

Cross Wind

Exactly the same procedure is used here as with an onshore
breeze, except that there is less urgency to get the centreboard
down. The sheets should be brought on about half way
and the centreboard lowered as soon as possible. If any drift
is made, it will be across the beach, not directly back onto
it as in the former case.

Offshore Breeze

The danger here, in a strong breeze, is of gybing or capsizing
before the skipper and crew have had time to orientate
themselves. However, sailing off on an offshore breeze is
not really difficult in moderate or light breezes.

In a strong offshore breeze, the boat should be put into
the water and turned to face the beach until the crew are
aboard and settled. There is no need to worry about the
centreboard, as the boat will be running and a deep
centreboard is not necessary.

Once the crew is aboard, the skipper allows her head to
fall off, and jumps aboard himself, letting the boat drift

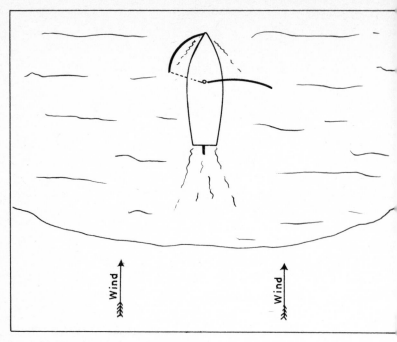

FIG 13 **Sailing a dinghy off the beach—
offshore breeze**

away from the beach. He should then quickly organise his
crew for the run out into open water.

Naturally all these conditions of launching and preparing
a boat can be altered by adverse weather. In very strong
winds a boat of any size can become unmanageable,
particularly when beginning to sail, when a sudden gust
can whip down and cause damage before she has gained
sufficient momentum, or before her crew are properly settled.

When this happens the only solution is for the skipper
and crew to be particularly thorough in their preparations
and be ready for any adverse conditions. If possible it is
wise even to wait a few minutes for the chance of a lull
to get the boat out into clear water. Once there, any wrongs
can be righted.

Chapter 3 **The Sailing Positions**

To understand the full complicated relationship between
aerodynamics and hydrodynamics which enable a boat to
be propelled by wind alone, one would need to study naval
architecture at length. It is not proposed to do so in this
volume. Sufficient at this stage for the beginner to have
a broad, basic knowledge of how a boat sails in order to
assist him to visualise the various forces at work under
differing sailing conditions. At this stage only the very
broadest outline will suffice, as confusion may be induced
instead of understanding.

There are a number of different factors involved in causing
a boat to sail, but principally the shape of the sail itself
is the most important. Unlike the celluloid models sold to
youngsters, the sail of a proper sail boat is not flat. It has

The shape of the sail gives it drive

quite a deep curve (called a *belly*) which enables it to form a concave surface (convex on the other side) when filled with wind.

When examined in cross section, the shape of the sail bears a remarkable resemblance to the cross section of the wing of an aeroplane and it is, in fact, designed in much the same way.

When a plane gathers speed along a runway the shape of the wing causes the wind to exert an uplift which takes the aircraft off the ground. If one could imagine that wing turned to the vertical, rather than the horizontal, one has a picture rather like a sail. The shape of the sail creates a sideways pressure, rather than an uplift, which pushes the boat forward and to one side. If a keel is added to prevent the sideways drift, the boat will move forward.

Of course, this shape of the sail applies principally when the wind is ahead, just as with the aircraft moving forward. At other times the sail is allowed to form a somewhat different shape—a larger belly, for example when the wind is astern, so that more wind can be gathered up to push the boat along.

In addition to the driving effect of the sail shape, another effect is achieved when two sails are used in conjunction (i.e., the jib and the main). In order to drive the boat forward into the wind the two sails are hauled in close to the boat so that between them there is a funnel-like gap. This is known in nautical terms as a *slot*. This slot causes the wind from the jib to be driven between itself and the mainsail and pushed out astern somewhat like a jet. This slot effect helps drive the boat forward into the wind.

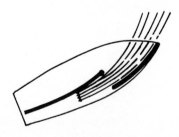

FIG 14 **Slot-effect**

**Illustrating the slot-effect between
the sails**

Of course the boat cannot go directly into the wind. If
it were to do so, the concave/convex shape of the sail would
not be able to form on either side and the sail would collapse.
The wind must always strike the sail at an angle, and in
most cases the angle at which a boat can sail closest to
the wind is 45 degrees, or four points from the wind itself.
Some of the higher-tuned boats, such as the racing twelve
metres, can point higher into the wind, but for an average
racing cruising vessel 45 degrees is a fairly good angle.

As mentioned just now, in order to drive the boat forward
when sailing into the wind, even at an angle of 45 degrees,
the sails must be hauled in close to the boat to create this
'slot-effect'. The term *close-hauled* is given to a boat which
is sailing as close to the wind as possible.

Whereas the sails are close into the boat when sailing
into the wind, exactly the reverse applies to a vessel with
the wind behind. Here the simple practice of sticking out
as much sail as possible to catch as much breeze as possible
holds good, and the sails are let out as far as they will
go, so that they are almost at right angles to the boat. This

WI ND

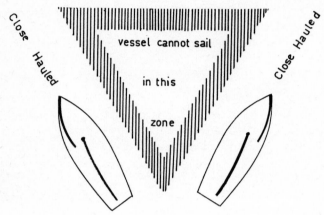

Close Hauled

Close Hauled

vessel cannot sail

in this

zone

TACK

TACK

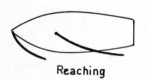

Reaching

Reaching

STARBOARD

PORT

Running Free

FIG 15 **The sailing positions—the boat can sail in a direct line anywhere around the compass except in the 'wind zone'**

is the time when spinnakers are set, cheaters come out, and even handkerchiefs may be strung out if they can achieve any effect! In short, when *running* before the wind, all sail is set! The term given to this condition is *running free*.

So, to recapitulate briefly, sails are pulled close into the boat when sailing into the wind. When sailing with the wind astern, sails are loosed right out. And, logically, when sailing with the wind anywhere between these two points, the sails are adjusted correspondingly. When the wind is on the beam (halfway from ahead to astern) the sails are set half way between right in and right out. When the wind is on the quarter (*almost* running) the sails are *almost* right out. This is a broad general rule, but it gives the beginner an immediate idea as to where the sails should be in relation to wind direction.

When the wind is on the beam, the condition is called *reaching*. If it is slightly before the beam (but not so much that the boat is close-hauled) it is termed *shy-reaching*. If a little aft of the beam (but not right astern) it is termed *broad-reaching*. Correct setting of the sails for different wind conditions is the art of the good sailor, and can only come with experience.

Luffing

As already described, the luff of a sail is the front, or leading edge. Since it is the first part of the sail to feel the effect of the wind, it is also the first indication that a sail is not set properly or the boat is not sailing properly. When this is the case, the wind destroys the clean-cut edge of the sail and it begins to flutter. This is called *Luffing*.

When sailing into the wind, the exact angle at which the boat will sail is difficult to judge by eye, and it must be manoeuvred a little until the luff of the jib begins to flutter. The boat is then luffing and sailing too close to the wind for maximum effect, so her head is brought away from the wind until the luffing stops.

When the jib luffs in the close-hauled condition it cannot be corrected by bringing on the sheets, as the sheets should already be as tight as possible. When reaching or running, however, the sheets are not tight and the luffing may be eliminated not by adjusting the ship's head, but simply by tightening the sheets. This, in fact, is the way the very maximum power is derived from any sail under any wind condition or direction. In practice therefore:

Maximum effect from any sail is achieved by easing it as far out as possible without luffing.

Note that this applies to *any* sail. It applies equally to jib, main and spinnaker.

A popular centreboarder

Chapter 4 Sailing the Boat

The previous chapter described briefly the way in which a boat sails, and the way in which the sails are adjusted for differing wind conditions. In this chapter we shall put theory into practice and sail the boat under close-hauled, running and reaching conditions.

In chapter 2 we have already prepared the boat and hoisted the sails. We are now in clear water and preparing to sail off. Obviously our first move is to find out just where the wind is coming from. This creates some difficulty for beginners, and the most satisfactory solution is to tie small pieces of wool or ribbon on the shrouds and backstay. These are known as *telltales* and as their name indicates, they tell the direction of the wind. This is only an approximate direction as the telltales will be affected by the movement of the boat through the wind, but it is sufficient to get an idea of where the wind is coming from.

Some boat owners prefer to fly flags or pennants from the top of the mast and use these as telltales. There is nothing wrong with the practice, apart from the fact that after many hours of sailing one tends to get a crick in the neck from looking upwards all the time.

Having ascertained the wind direction, the next move is to consider this direction in relation to our course. We will have decided on a destination and, mentally at least, turned the boat in that direction. If, when pointing towards our destination the wind is ahead, or to be precise, dead ahead, then the yacht will not sail towards it. The sails will flap and the boat will not move, apart perhaps, from drifting astern. But if our destination is not in the same direction as the wind, indeed more than forty-five degrees from the direction of the wind, then by setting the sails correctly, the boat will sail directly towards it.

WIND

FIG 16 **Close hauled**

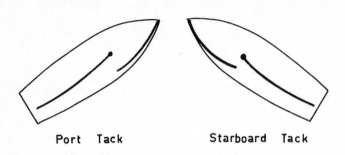

Port   Tack   Starboard   Tack

In short, a sailboat will sail in a direct line anywhere round the compass except in the 90 degree zone, 45 degrees of which lie on either side of the wind (see Fig. 15).

Sailing close-hauled

Assuming that our destination is in such a position (about 45 degrees off the wind) that we can sail straight towards it close-hauled. The procedure would then be as follows:

1. Drop the centreboard.
2. Bring on the sheets as hard as possible.
3. Up tiller to take the boat's head away from the wind until the sails fill. Experiment to ensure that the sails are not luffing when the boat is heading for the destination. If luffing occurs she must be eased away from the wind and can then only reach the destination by tacking.
4. As she gathers way, the boat will try to round up into the wind with every gust. This is corrected by bringing the tiller up until she is back on course, and may require constant adjustment through the passage.
5. Continue sailing, watching the jib all the time in case luffing begins.

Tacking

If the destination lies directly in the direction of the wind, or anywhere within the 90-degree zone in which the boat cannot sail direct, then she must resort to *tacking*.

38

Assuming we are attempting to sail directly into the wind, the nearest point at which we can sail without luffing is 45 degrees to the wind. If the wind is coming over the starboard side we are said to be on a *starboard tack*, while the reverse is the case if we are on a *port tack*. Assuming we are *close-hauled on a starboard tack*, we are sailing with the wind coming over the starboard side at an angle of approximately 45 degrees to our course. Obviously if we continue in this direction we shall make a certain amount of progress towards our destination, but we will not finally reach it on this tack.

Having sailed some way on a starboard tack then, we go about onto a port tack. Sailing *close-hauled on a port tack*, we will make further progress towards our objective, although again we will not be sailing directly towards it.

Tacking hard to windward

Later we will have to go about on a starboard tack again.

By repeating this process, the boat makes a zig-zag progress directly into the wind and towards our objective. This is known as tacking.

The critical part of tacking is to know just when to go about and make another tack. By tacking too far on one tack we will waste time and direction, and by tacking too frequently we shall waste time also, as too much going about slows the progress of the boat. Broadly speaking, the best time to go about and make a new tack is when the objective is on our beam. If it is ahead of the beam then we are progressing towards it, albeit not directly. If it is abaft the beam we are not making progress towards it, in fact we are going away from it.

By tacking when the object is on the beam, we should, theoretically, be able to sail directly towards it. But this is not so in practice because of drift, or *leeway* as it is termed, which causes the boat to slide sideways through the water. But, by going about with the objective on the beam, even though we may not point directly towards it, we will progress at the maximum rate possible under the circumstances (see Fig. 17).

**Tacking hard with the trapeze
crew out**

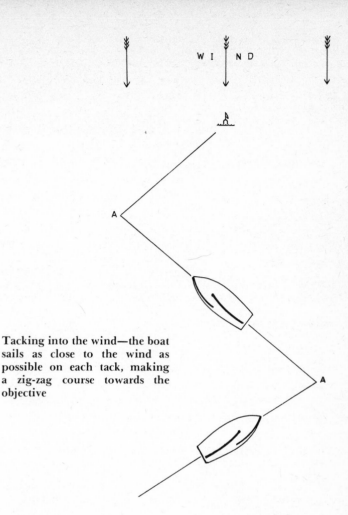

WIND

FIG 17 Tacking into the wind—the boat sails as close to the wind as possible on each tack, making a zig-zag course towards the objective

It is important to remember that although a boat may sail on a starboard or port *tack* with the wind anywhere, it is only when she is carrying out this zig-zag manoeuvre with the idea of sailing into the wind that the term *tacking* is used. *Working* or *beating* are other terms given to this procedure. Thus the term *dead beat to windward*.

Reaching

If the destination is across wind, i.e., the wind is on or nearly on the beam, the boat can sail directly towards it. The procedure then is as follows:

41

Reaching is the fastest sailing position

1. Point the boat's head towards the destination, at the same time easing the sheets.

2. Once on course continue to ease the sheets until the sails begin to luff. Take them on again until luffing has stopped, thus achieving maximum effect.

3. Raise the centreboard about half way.

4. If, at any stage, a sail begins to luff, take on the sheet a little. If, judging by the telltales, the wind moves round towards the stern, ease the sheets a little. Shy-reaching or broad-reaching require these adjustments to the sheets (see Fig. 18).

Running

As with reaching, the boat can sail directly towards her destination if the wind is astern. The procedure is as follows:

1. Point the boat's head towards the destination. Ease the sheets right out or until the sails luff. If the wind is dead astern the sheets should be eased right out without any sign of luffing.

2. If the jib collapses (by virtue of the main blanketing it from the wind), it can be hauled across on the windward

42

WIND

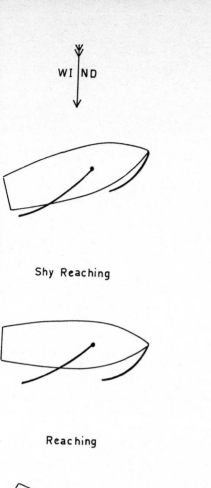

Shy Reaching

Reaching

Broad Reaching

FIG 18 **Reaching**

WIND

with Spinnaker

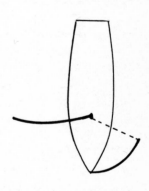

with Goosewing Jib

FIG 19 **Running free**

43

side, where it will fill again. The spinnaker pole (or whisker pole in a dinghy) can be used to keep it in place. This is known as a goosewing jib.

    3.   Raise the centreboard all the way.

    4.   If required, drop the jib and set the spinnaker.

    5.   When running free under conditions such as those described in this section, there exists a danger of the boat *gybing*. This happens when the wind moves past the stern of the boat to a position where it can reach the lee side of the mainsail. In small boats an unexpected gybe will frequently cause a capsize. In larger boats considerable damage to gear and sails may be sustained.

Running 'Goosewinged'

Going about and gybing

When the wind moves from one side to the other the boat
is said to be changing tack. This involves changing the
course and changing the sails onto the opposite side. It can
be done in two ways, and usually the way chosen is that
which makes the shortest distance of the change in course.

Say, for example, the vessel is headed close-hauled on
a starboard tack, and (in working to windward) needs to
become close-hauled on a port tack. This will involve a
change of direction of about 90 degrees, by going about
into the wind. Gybing would not be in order here as gybing
would involve a swing through some 270 degrees.

Similarly, if a change onto a port tack is required when
running before the wind it would be far quicker to gybe
through 90 or 100 degrees than swing up into wind, go
about and fall off the wind, an arc of perhaps 200 or 300
degrees.

Basically, then, it can be accepted that when going into
the wind a vessel changes tack by going about. When running
before the wind, by gybing. However, there are exceptions
to this, particularly in the case of gybing, which can be
a difficult and dangerous manoeuvre in heavy weather. In
this case going about may be preferable from a safety point
of view, even if it involves a far greater distance.

Going about

When the helmsman decides the time has come to go about,
he warns his crew, 'Ready About'. Immediately this warning
has been given, he puts the helm hard down and the boat
swings up into the wind. The sails flap, and then the jib
is 'backed', i.e., the wind veers round to its opposite side.

The order then is 'Lee-Oh', at which the crew release
and take on sheets in order to bring the sails over to the
opposite side. In small dinghies the order 'Lee-Oh' is often
given as the helm goes down. Being light and manoeuvrable,
they spin around with their own momentum. Larger vessels,
however, need the added push of the jib backed the wrong
way in order to make a fast turn, particularly when racing,
and wait for the jib to back before calling 'Lee-Oh'.

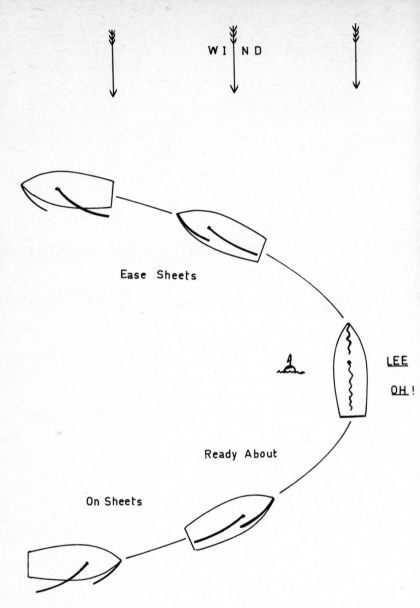

WIND

Ease Sheets

LEE
OH !

Ready About

On Sheets

FIG 20 **Going about**

In order to drive the boat hard up into the wind and make a fast turn, the sheets must be hard on at the moment of putting down the helm. Thus many skippers automatically order 'On sheets', prior to 'Ready about'.

**Layout of a modern fibreglass
yacht**

Gybing

Gybing is a more difficult manoeuvre and is not
recommended for beginners until they have put some
experience under their belts. In light conditions it is fairly
easy, but in heavy winds it can cause some difficulty and
damage. Basically, going about is done into the wind, and
gybing with the wind astern. It is a broad truth that gybing
is going about with the wind behind.

The problem with gybing arises from the fact that the
boom is right out, i.e., the sheets are eased due to the wind
being astern. When the wind gets on the lee side of the
mainsail, the sail and boom are thrown right across the
boat to the same position on the opposite side, a distance
of some 180 degrees. This does not arise when going about,
as with the sheets on and the boom hauled close into the
boat, it only has a short distance to travel before the wind
gets to the other side of the sail.

To minimise the effect of this rush of the boom across
the boat when gybing, a condition close to that of going
about should be arrived at before the gybe begins. Thus,

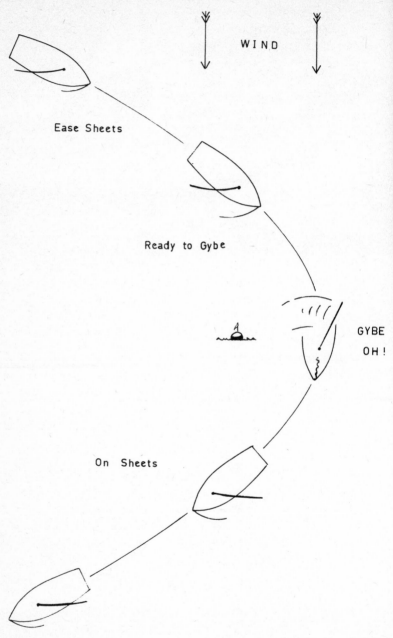

WIND

Ease Sheets

Ready to Gybe

GYBE
OH!

On Sheets

FIG 21 **Gybing**

48

the main boom is brought in close so that at the actual moment of gybing it has only a short distance to travel across the boat. And once over the other side it can be eased out to the position required.

The procedure then, is for the skipper to warn his crew 'Ready to Gybe'. He pulls the helm up, and at the same time orders the main sheet to be pulled hard on. When the boom goes over it is 'Gybe-Oh' and the main is eased out on the other side fairly quickly to absorb the shock of the wind as it hits the other side.

If this manoeuvre is to be done without any banging or lurching, good co-ordination between skipper and mainsheet hand is required.

Because of the lightness of their booms, small boats and dinghies do not need to be so cautious. In fact they *do not pull on the main sheet at all,* but simply let it flick from one side to the other, helping with a push if need be.

The diagrams accompanying this section will perhaps enable the novice to understand better the location of the wind both in going about and in gybing, for the wind decides which of these two methods should be used to change tack.

Sailing Round the Compass

Having grasped the fundamentals of sail setting for different directions of wind, the beginner should start to sail his boat in every possible direction—*round the compass.* Start by heading for a specific point somewhere along the shore of the bay, setting the sails so that the boat can sail directly to that point.

Let's assume it is a starboard reach (i.e., the wind is coming over the starboard side of the beam). After a few moments' sailing on this course to get the feel of the boat, select another spot, say about 50 degrees to the left of the first, and bring the boat round to head for it. This will involve easing the sails, as the wind will now be coming round astern. At once a basic rule can be applied to all forms of sailing.

When altering course closer to the wind. On Sheets. When altering course farther away from the wind, Ease Sheets.

49

By this time we are sailing on a broad reach, the wind now coming over the starboard quarter, and the sails are eased out, but not right out as yet.

Now select another point a further 20 or 30 degrees to the left of the last and head for it. Again we are coming away from the wind. Again we will 'Ease Sheets'.

Now we are running dead down wind and the sails are right out as far as they will go. The jib has probably collapsed as it is blanketed by the main, but there is no worry about that.

Select another point some 30 degrees or so to the left

**Sailing in light airs can
be frustrating**

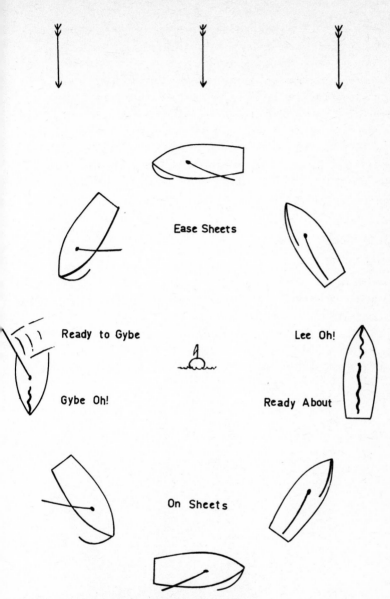

FIG 22 **Sailing round the compass**

again and alter course to steer for it. Now we are altering course more *into* the wind, therefore, the sails come on ... 'On sheets'.

51

We are reaching to port now, and we select another point, say about 50 or 60 degrees to the left. We are coming into the wind so we bring the sheets on. But, what's this? Suddenly the sails are flapping violently. We are luffing.

In altering course 50 or 60 degrees from our reaching point, we cam up into the wind too far—past the 45 degree angle that our boat will sail into the wind, so that she luffs. We are in the non-sailing zone—too high into the wind, so that we have no option but to bring the helm up and pull her head off the wind until the luffing stops. We are now close-hauled to port.

To go any farther to the left will involve entering the non-sailing zone again, so we will have to change tack. Since we are pointing into the wind, this means going about.

Now we are close-hauled on the starboard tack, and to return to our original point from which we started we shall have to ease sheets a little until she is reaching to starboard again. We have now sailed *round the compass*.

Taking it in easy stages like this, the beginner will soon grasp the fundamental handling of the boat. But it is not sufficient just to move in short, consecutive stages as described

Working to windward

above. Now try altering course over 80 or 100 degrees, even 180 degrees in one manoeuvre.

For example, set the boat on a starboard reach, and alter course through 180 degrees to starboard, thus bringing her onto a port reach.

This will require the following procedures:

'On sheets', to bring her up into the wind.

'Ready about', to change tack.

'Ease sheets', to take her to the reaching position.

Another example. Set the boat running free on a starboard tack and alter course so that she is close-hauled to port.

'Ready to gybe', to change tack.

'On sheets', until she is close-hauled.

In this last case, there is an alternative, as the change of course is approximately 180 degrees. The following would be equally correct:

'On sheets', to bring her to the close-hauled position.

'Ready about', to change tack.

These are but a few examples of the type of manoeuvring that will be required of a helmsman before he can be sufficiently confident to take a boat into a race. Remember that in the close confines of a race it will be more than simply altering course as there will be many other boats around to complicate the issue.

The course round which a yacht race travels may vary according to the location and circumstances of wind and tide. But generally the committee try if possible to design the course in such a way that the boats will be required to sail through every form of sailing, from the dead beat to windward, to reaching and running and, if possible, gybing round a mark. The Olympic course used for most international and national races is a triangle at least one leg of which is dead to windward. Sailing such a course involves the use of every point of sailing.

Chapter 5 **Spinnakers**

Spinnakers differ from other sails in a number of ways. First, they are not attached to the boat down one edge, but fly freely with only the three corners attached. Second, they are *extras* to a boat's wardrobe, i.e., they can only be flown under certain conditions. Third, they require a considerable amount of accessory gear.

Even among themselves spinnakers vary considerably. Some are full cut (balloon type) and some are flat, some made from heavy material, and some are gossamer-light. They even vary from boat to boat, and in offering the student a basic grounding in spinnaker work, this chapter is based purely on a broad average of boats, both in the dinghy classes and larger, ocean racing boats.

The principal difficulty arising from the use of the

**A big spinnaker can quickly
get out of hand**

spinnaker lies in its size. Usually a spinnaker is much larger in area than any other sail on the boat, and almost invariably of a lighter material. This makes it a very flighty thing to have up on deck and to sort out so that it will fly cleanly and without any twists or hitches.

For this reason, the basic essential in preparing for spinnaker work is to have all the various ropes and pieces laid out in clear untangled form. Likewise the spinnaker should be folded into a washing basket or some similar container, so that when hoisted it will come out neatly and not all hocus-pocus.

The spinnaker is similar to other sails in that it has three corners; peak, clew and tack. In most cases the clew and tack are identical and interchangeable, making for ease in gybing. The peak is always identified by a colour patch. This may be part of the colour design or just a small patch sewn onto the peak for identification.

When preparing the spinnaker, it should be neatly flaked into the basket, leaving the clew and the tack sticking out, so that it lies carefully laid in swathes from the foot to the peak, which should be on the top of the basket.

Some yachtsmen prefer to 'stop up' the spinnaker into a large, sausage shape. This has many advantages. It does not fill with wind when being hoisted, and does not catch on crosstrees or spreaders. However, this is a matter of personal taste.

To stop up a spinnaker it must be taken down below and stretched along the cabin. The tack and clew are brought together and the sail folded in on itself until it has been rolled quite tightly.

It is then secured in place by *one* round of medium grade knitting wool, about three feet down from the peak. The folding process is continued throughout the length of the spinnaker with wool stops (only *one* round) about every four to six feet. When the foot is reached a *double* turn of wool is made as a precaution against unexpected breaking out. The sail will resemble a long sausage, and should be folded in the basket with the clew and tack out, and the peak on the top, as mentioned before.

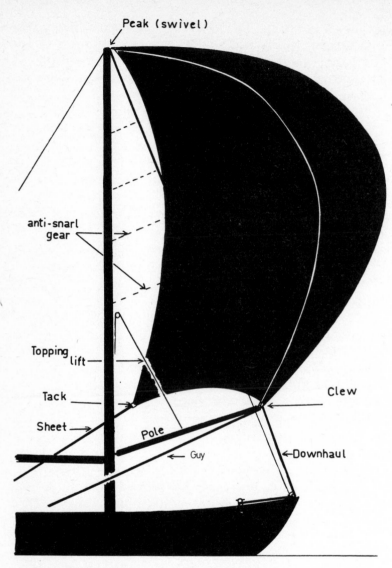

Peak (swivel)

anti-snarl gear

Topping lift

Tack

Sheet

Pole

Guy

Clew

Downhaul

FIG 23 Spinnaker gear

When the spinnaker is set the peak is attached to a halyard and hoisted in the normal way. The tack, however, is not secured—as with the other sails—to the boat, but pushed out on the end of the *spinnaker pole*—a specially designed pole with matching clips at each end. The pole is controlled by a rope called the *guy*. The clew, as with other sails, is controlled by the sheet.

To facilitate gybing, most larger boats have sheets and guys of identical rope which are interchangeable.

Other parts of spinnaker gear are the *downhaul* or *kicker*, used to tie the pole down to the boat and prevent it being pulled up by the sail, and the *topping lift*, which is used to take the weight of the pole.

All sheets and guys for the spinnaker are set outside the rigging.

To set up and hoist the spinnaker, then, the forward hands (at least two on yachts, one in dinghies) must be very conversant with the gear. Once everything is ready on the foredeck, the procedure is then as follows:

1. Pass the sheet from forward down the leeward side back to the cockpit, keeping it outside all rigging and other sheets. Clip the forward end onto the clew of the sail.

2. Pass the brace down the windward side in a similar manner, and clip onto the tack of the sail.

3. Clear the halyards and pass the hoisting part round the forestay and under the jib (if flying). Clip onto the peak. The spinnaker can then be hauled up behind the jib, which prevents it from filling with wind until properly in position.

4. Clip the inboard end of the spinnaker pole to the ring on the mast, and secure the topping lift. To the outboard end clip on the tack (together with guy) and the downhaul.

5. Take the weight of the spinnaker pole with the topping lift, until the former is horizontal. Make fast the topping lift.

6. Secure the tail of the downhaul so that it does not fly over the side. The spinnaker is now ready to hoist.

7. Hoist away on the halyard until the peak is at the top. Make fast. The sail will flap in the lee of the jib.

8. Take the weight on the guy, and work out the pole until it is roughly in line with the main boom. Tighten the downhaul and make fast.

9. Take the weight on the sheet. This will break out the spinnaker (if stopped) and fill it with wind.

A large crew is required when
flying a big spinnaker

10.   Adjust sheets and guys until maximum effect is
obtained.

N.B.   The sheet must *never* be taken on until guys and
downhaul are made fast. Since the sheet fills the sail with
wind, considerable damage may be sustained if everything
is not secure before the weight of the spinnaker comes onto
the various gear.

The art of flying a spinnaker—as with any sail—is to
keep it drawing at its maximum. This, too, is achieved by
easing the sheet as far as possible without luffing. Where

a sail such as the jib is attached to a stay, it is possible
to make the necessary adjustments before securing the sheet.
With a spinnaker this is not the case. As it is not attached
to a stay, the spinnaker will luff so severely that it will
more than likely collapse altogether, and for this reason
the sheet can never be secured, but must be played all the
time, rather as though one were flying a kite. Hence the
nickname yachtsmen have given the spinnaker—*The Kite*.

How to fly a spinnaker under different conditions; the
types of spinnaker to carry, and when to set a certain
spinnaker, are a few of the many involved questions
concerned in spinnaker work. These can really only be
resolved according to individual requirements, as spinnakers
are usually cut to suit a specific boat and not as a stock
item.

The main feature of spinnaker work is experience, and
furthermore experience with one particular boat and its
spinnakers. The following hints are offered only as general
guidance for the beginner, and not as hard and fast rules
when using a spinnaker.

1. The position of the spinnaker boom will vary
according to wind conditions and individual boats. But

FIG 24 **Spinnaker boom positions**

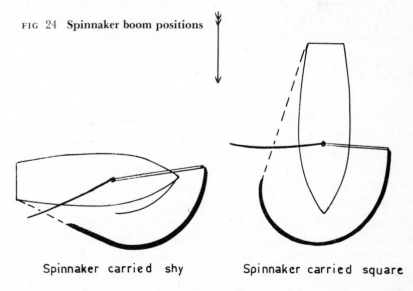

Spinnaker carried shy   Spinnaker carried square

generally it should be set as a continuation of the main boom.

2. Following this theory, the boom is moved forward as the boat rounds more into the wind, and *squared off* as the boat commences to run before the wind (i.e., the opposite to the main boom).

3. Although some spinnakers are so cut that they may be flown closer to the wind than average, a spinnaker is usually only set when the wind is abeam or abaft the beam. On the beam it is known as a *shy* spinnaker.

4. The leads for the sheets and guys will need to be adjusted according to the shape of the boat and size of the spinnaker. A sailmaker or rigger should be consulted about this.

5. The spinnaker is a big sail which can become extremely heavy on the sheet hand. It is usual in larger boats to lead the spinnaker sheet onto one of the cockpit winches, so that it can be 'played' via the winch.

Handing the Spinnaker

The all-important thing in handing, or dropping the spinnaker is to release the sheet before anything else, so as to spill the wind and relieve the strain on the gear. There are then two systems of dropping the spinnaker, each of which has its advantages. Both will be described here.

SYSTEM ONE

1. Let go the sheet. The sail will collapse.

2. Let go the guy, allowing the pole to lie fore and aft.

3. Lower the sail, one forward hand attending to the halyard, while the other pulls the sail down into the basket on the foredeck.

4. Once down and stowed, remove all the other gear.

The advantage of this system is that when all attachments are unclipped, the sail is in the basket with three corners out, all ready to go up again—a useful asset where short distances are sailed. The main disadvantage is that the spinnaker must be taken off some time before reaching the rounding mark in a race, otherwise when the boat rounds up into the wind, the spinnaker will become unmanageable and wrap itself around the foredeck gear, as well as the foredeck hands!

SYSTEM TWO

1. Let go the tack. The sail will now fly from the top of the mast.
2. Lower the halyard and at the same time haul the sail into the cockpit via the sheet.
3. Remove all other gear.

The advantage here is the speed with which the spinnaker can be dropped, and the fact that the boat can be sailing into the wind from the moment the clew is released. The disadvantage is in having to sort out the spinnaker and take it forward ready for the next turn.

Gybing the Spinnaker

It is not possible to go about with the spinnaker flying, but it is possible to tack without taking it down by gybing around. Again, there are a number of different ways of gybing a spinnaker, but the basic method used on most larger vessels is described here.

Approaching the gybing position:

1. Unclip the spinnaker pole from the tack, taking care not to unclip the brace.
2. Swing the pole across to the opposite side (the topping lift may have to be adjusted to do this) and clip onto the clew.

FIG 25 **Gybing the spinnaker**

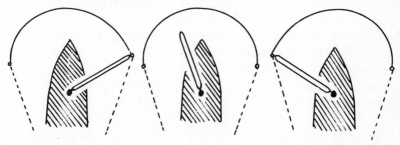

3.   When the boat gybes, the clew becomes the tack (thus the guy becomes the sheet) and vice versa.

If done properly this gybe can be carried out smoothly without collapsing the spinnaker during the time that the pole is not connected and flying from only guy and sheet. Obviously, it is necessary to have a spinnaker pole that will pass inside the forestay. If not, the pole will have to be unclipped at the mast and brought inboard to clear the stay.

A well-gybed spinnaker is a delight to a yachtsman's eye, but it is a manoeuvre that requires much practice, as one small slip can make the delight a hideous, tangled mess.

The Death Roll

Much has been made of the so-called *death roll* which besets ocean racing yachts when under spinnaker. Basically what happens is that the yacht, running downwind with spinnaker up and full main out the other side, begins to yaw on the following seas.

This sets up a roll which is aggravated by the alternating pressure of wind in the spinnaker as she rolls to windward, and the main as she rolls to leeward. The roll increases as sea and wind effects synchronise to the point where, unless it is stopped, the yacht will roll to windward and dip her spinnaker pole into the sea. This drags the spinnaker down into the water, it fills, and the strain is enormous. If the spinnaker is attached to the top of the mast, chances are that the top of the mast will be pulled off. Even if no structural damage is sustained, the boat is pulled up to a standing halt, and a long process of cutting away must be started before she can get under way again.

Although it is very difficult to prevent the roll developing, it can often be corrected by easing the spinnaker sheet before the roll develops to the extreme stage.

Chapter 6 Handling the Boat

At this point the student has now learned to handle his boat through all basic phases of sailing. From here on, he will adapt this basic knowledge to the many forms and facets of sailing which will occur as he travels across the water. Needless to say, there are hundreds of different manoeuvres he may be called upon to perform, many of them quite common, some common only to the water or conditions in which he sails.

The less common ones will test his skill and ability, and only practice will enable him to perform them correctly. In this chapter some of the more common manoeuvres are described, as a guide to the sort of thing the yachtsman encounters in the everyday process of sailing.

Sailing off a Mooring

This can be a tricky manoeuvre, particularly if the moorings of other craft lie close at hand, and there is little manoeuvring room. It should not therefore be attempted until the helmsman and his crew are fully familiar with their vessel and her performance under differing conditions. Sailing off a mooring is made more difficult by the fact that in sheltered spots—normal mooring areas—the wind has a tendency to fluctuate both in strength and direction. With expensive boats moored close at hand on either side this fluctuating wind can make it a nerve-wracking business trying to sail off a mooring without risking damage to the nearby carft.

It is better at first to use the engine to clear the moorings, and then practise sailing on and off another mooring in less crowded conditions, until satisfied that it can be done efficiently and without risk. While there are a number of so-called purists who deride the use of an engine on board a yacht, these are a minority who seek only to boost their own egotism. Whilst not detracting in any way from the polished and attractive performance of an experienced helmsman carrying out difficult mooring manoeuvres, safety comes first in yachting, and only when that vast store of knowledge and experience has been gained can the helmsman afford to cast a disdainful eye on the engine.

How much better to motor through the moorings, albeit with red ears, than reach for one's insurance policy with a very red face!

Assuming, however, that the skipper and crew have reached the point where they are sufficiently experienced to try this manoeuvre, then the following is the method adopted:

Lying to the mooring, the boat is stationary and head to wind, unless the current is stronger than the wind, when she will lie head to current.

In the Northern Hemisphere the tidal stream tends to be stronger than prevailing winds while the reverse is true in southern climes. However, tidal effect is dealt with in more detail later in this chapter. In order to be able to manoeuvre the boat, she must be moving through the water, as the rudder does not operate until water flows past it. In order to obtain this movement through the water, the boat's head must fall off the wind at least 45 degrees to reach her closest sailing position.

It is here that the problems arise. Before reaching her sailing position and beginning to gain momentum, the wind strikes the hull and pushes it sideways. Thus, before the boat has had time to start moving and come under control, she has been pushed sideways into the next craft. It is necessary, therefore, to have the sails drawing and the boat actually ready to manoeuvre before the mooring is released. Even better, it is preferable to have the boat swung round and pointing clear of all other craft when the mooring is dropped. Fig. 26 illustrates this manoeuvre.

The sails are hoisted and set. Then the procedure is as follows:

1. Back the jib, leaving the main sheet still free. This causes the boat's head to be forced off the wind. She will

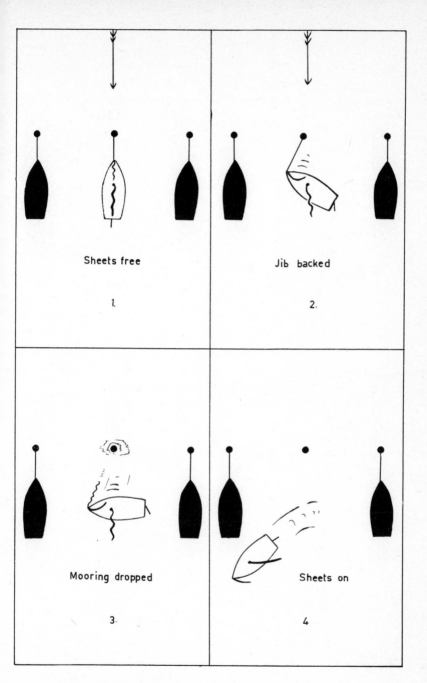

FIG 26 **Sailing off a mooring**

**Small centreboarders make
exciting sailing**

continue to swing sideways, dragging the mooring chain
with her.

2. Let go the mooring. Jib still backed, main still free.
By this time she will have swung well round, but the jib

still backed ensures that she will continue to swing and not make any forward progress towards other boats. The moment of letting go the mooring must be judged by the strain on the mooring cable. There will come a point where the cable will not stretch any further, and unless released, will pull the boat's head back into the wind.

3. When her bow has swung well clear, release the jib and take on both jib and mainsheets on their correct sides. The boat will now start to move forward and come under control.

If the moorings are exceptionally close together, the boat can be swung further round by walking the mooring aft, as she is swinging. This will have the effect of swinging the boat right round 180 degrees to the point where she is virtually moored by the stern. The mooring can then be released.

Tide

If the tide is stronger than the wind the boat will lie head to tide and not head to wind. Here a considerable amount of judgment is required. If the wind is strong enough, the sheets can be taken on and the boat sailed straight ahead, dropping the mooring as she goes. If not, the sheets must remain slack and the vessel's head swung off the mooring by the rudder. Remember that the tide or current will cause a flow of water over the rudder so that it is effective even though the boat is stationary. Once her head is swung off, the boat can be sailed (if there is room) or the mooring can be dropped and the boat allowed to drift astern with the tide until clear of other craft. There are many combinations of wind and tide which can affect this manoeuvre, and practice is the only solution to most of them. Likewise, good co-ordination between crew (particularly the forward hand who handles the mooring) and skipper are essential.

Sailing onto a Mooring

This is not nearly as difficult a manoeuvre as sailing off the mooring, as the boat is under way and, therefore, under

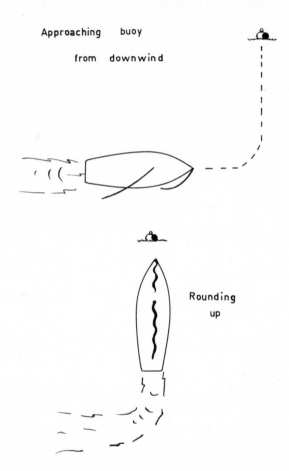

A

Approaching   buoy

from   downwind

B

Rounding
up

FIG 27 **Sailing onto a mooring**

control when approaching the mooring. If a mistake is made
or weather conditions make things difficult, it is simple
merely to ease sheets and go round again.

   In order to pick up the mooring the boat must be moving
very slowly so that it will be almost stationary at the moment

she reaches the buoy. If she were to sail right onto the mooring, the forward hand, in grabbing the buoy and trying to check the boat's momentum, would most likely go over the side. Even if he managed to get a turn around the bollard, the weight of the boat at speed would break the mooring cable.

The boat must be brought close to the mooring and then rounded up into the wind, with all sheets loose so that her momentum carries her on to the buoy. Judgment is required to ensure that in rounding up, the momentum will carry her to the buoy at the moment she loses way and not overshoot too fast.

Here again the emphasis is on knowing one particular boat. Every boat performs differently, and one will carry her way for some yards after rounding up into the wind, while another will stop almost immediately. Again, tides can affect the approach, and some knowledge of how the tide is moving will have to be included in the skipper's analysis as he makes his approach.

The mooring may be approached from any direction, i.e., upwind or downwind, or—the ideal condition—acrosswind. But in every case the boat must be downwind of the buoy when she is rounded up for the final approach.

The step by step procedure is as follows:

1. Sail towards the buoy, aiming for a point some distance downwind of it. The actual distance can only be found by practice, as mentioned earlier, and is dependent on the speed of the boat and the distance she carries her way.

2. Approach this point sailing normally, then, when in the position dead downwind of the mooring buoy, put the helm hard down, 'Let Fly' all sheets, and round the boat up into the wind.

3. Watch the approach of the buoy as the boat loses way. If there is no chance of reaching it, or if she will overshoot, hard up tiller, 'On Sheets' and bring her off the wind to start sailing again. Gybe round and try again.

Some yachtsmen like to reduce sail before making their approach to the mooring, but unless weather is heavy, this can make things more difficult. It depends on the individual boat again, of course, but most yachts are designed to perform with a full suit of sails in normal weather, and to take off one sail can unbalance them and make them more difficult to handle.

Unless conditions are very bad, I think it is better to approach with full sail and have the boat under normal control. If the wind is strong it merely means the boat will have to be rounded up a little farther away from the buoy.

Once the mooring is taken aboard, there is no great hurry to drop the sails, provided the sheets are free. The boat will lie head to wind and the sails will flap idly until there is time to take them down.

Sailing up to a Jetty

Sailing up to a jetty, or any other object for that matter, requires exactly the same procedure as sailing onto a mooring. Obviously, the jetty must be in such a position in relation to the wind that the boat can be rounded up to it. It must also have sufficient water around it to allow for rounding up.

Be very careful, particularly when sailing off the jetty again, to ensure that the boat does not heel as the sheets come on, and foul her rigging or mast on the jetty. It can be most embarrassing, after an impressive approach, to sail off leaving mast and rigging on the jetty!

Picking up a Man Overboard

Picking up a person (or object) overboard again requires a similar technique to that described in picking up a mooring buoy. Here it is even more important that the rounding up is done correctly, for if a fast moving boat were to strike someone in the water, it might well kill them. Be on the safe side when making the approach and keep a few feet away from him. Unless he is unconscious he can swim the few feet and be dragged aboard.

If the person who goes overboard is a good swimmer it is sufficient just to round up into the wind and let the sheets fly. The boat will slow down, stop, and probably give the victim sufficient time to swim back, or at least

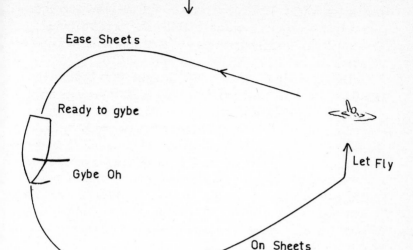

FIG 28 **Picking up a man overboard
(close hauled or reaching)**

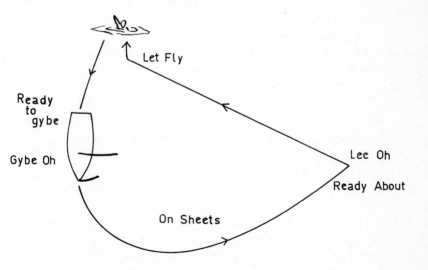

FIG 29 **Picking up a man overboard
(running free)**

grab a rope, before her head pays off. Remember the number one rule is to let go the sheets. With sheets freed the boat will not move far, even when her head pays off. With sheets on she will dart away the minute the sails fill.

If, however, the wind is too strong, or the man overboard is not a good swimmer or is unconscious, then it is better to gybe the boat around and pick him up. Note that it is quicker to gybe around; going about would put the boat upwind of him and she would have to be sailed to leeward to get into position for rounding up. By gybing round she is automatically in position downwind. (See Fig. 28).

If the man falls overboard when the boat is sailing dead downwind, she must be brought round on to the wind and tacked back upwind until in a position to make her approach. (See Fig. 29).

Heaving To

The term 'Heaving to' is generally thought of as being a means to ride out a storm. This is not so, and many a boat is hove to in quiet wind and water, so that the skipper and crew may enjoy a leisurely cup of tea, or make some minor repair.

Heaving to simply means stopping the boat and setting her up so that she remains stationary and in the most comfortable position, with her bow to wind and waves (not directly, but at a comfortable angle). In the days of big sailing ships, the captain hove to outside the entrance to a port to await a pilot, or when he met another ship and wished to exchange pleasantries. In those days the manoeuvre was accomplished by backing the upper sail against the lower. With modern fore and aft rigs the same effect is obtained by backing the foresail (jib) against the main.

The procedure for heaving to is as follows:

1. Round up into the wind as though to go about, but do not 'Lee-Oh' when the jib is backed.

2. When the jib is backed, put the helm hard down, bring the sheets hard on and secure everything.

Wait until the boat has settled down before making any slight adjustments to the sails. Under normal rig and in

**When sailing single-handed,
don't fall overboard!**

normal weather, no adjustment will be needed. The boat
will lie at a slight angle to wind and waves, with little
motion other than a slight drift to leeward. (See Fig. 30).

Heaving to is a useful manoeuvre in practice and one
can bring to mind a hundred uses, apart from comfort in

FIG 30 **Heaving to**

taking some refreshment. Standing by a disabled vessel, waiting for another boat to come up, waiting for the start of a race, or, simply for a few minutes' sunbaking. No matter what the reason, the boat will sit quietly without need of attention for as long as she is required to do so, and make only a slight drift to leeward.

Apart from good exercise when training a crew, the only reason for turning a sailboat in her own length is to impress someone. Even then it is only impressive when undertaken with a farily large yacht. Smaller dinghies swing around in their own length as a matter of course when manoeuvring, but then they are much more manageable and have short, fin keels to pivot on.

Turning a keel yacht in her own length is not easy, because normally she requires forward movement to make the rudder effective. However, the boat can be spun progressively into shorter and shorter circles, so that the action of sail and keel are almost continuous. The procedure is as follows:

1. Assuming the boat is sailing close-hauled, bring up the helm and lash it hard up. Ease sheets as her head falls off. The boat will go through a gybe and begin rounding up on the opposite tack.

2. Bring on the sheets as she does so and this will force her about on the other tack again.

3. Ease sheets immediately her head falls off and prepare for another gybe.

74

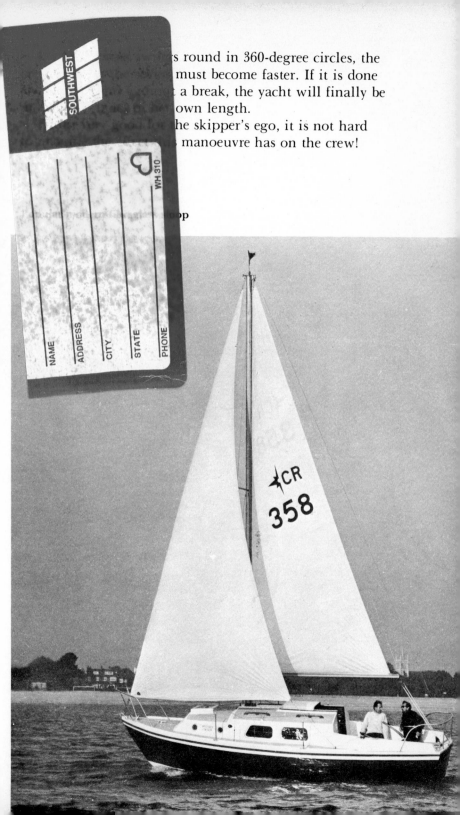

round in 360-degree circles, the
must become faster. If it is done
a break, the yacht will finally be
own length.

he skipper's ego, it is not hard
manoeuvre has on the crew!

Anchoring Under Sail

The correct way to anchor a yacht under sail depends once again on the manoeuvre, described earlier, for picking up a mooring buoy. The spot in which the yacht is to be anchored is approached, and the anchor prepared. Allowing for sufficient room on a lee shore, the skipper rounds her up into the wind until she loses way. The anchor is then dropped in the pre-planned position and the warp paid out as the boat's head falls off. Providing the sheets are free, she will not sail, but drift astern until sufficient warp is out, and she can be brought up.

This is the correct and seamanlike way to anchor, and providing it is for a short time, and the weather is fair, it is an efficient and attractive manoeuvre. However, if the yacht is to be anchored for some time or the weather prospects are not good, I like to know that my anchor has been driven hard home in the bottom and will not readily pull out.

To do this I employ a most unseamanlike manoeuvre and one which, perhaps, should not be mentioned in a book of this kind. However, I have yet to find anyone—even the most critical—who will deny its effectiveness.

FIG 31 **Anchoring**

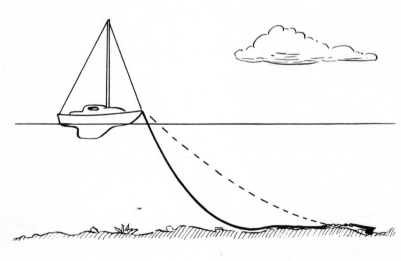

Sailing at night can be an interesting experience

In this case the boat is sailed downwind, and under reduced sail. When the point is reached at which the boat is to be placed, the anchor is dropped while still sailing downwind.

The boat is edged slightly to windward to prevent fouling the warp, but the sails remain full until the boat is brought up with a tremendous jerk as the limit of the warp is reached. This jerk has the twofold effect of driving home the anchor in the bottom, and rounding the boat head to wind.

The secret of anchoring a boat successfully lies in the length of warp let out. The warp acts as a spring by lying in a *bight* which absorbs any strain from the boat and avoids risk of pulling the anchor out. At least three to five times the depth of water should be allowed when estimating the amount of warp to let out.

Chapter 7   Balancing

When the wind heels a yacht, the pendulum effect of the weighted keel brings her back up to the upright position, or prevents her from heeling too far. With smaller boats and dinghies which do not have a weighted keel, the crew themselves must provide the righting lever.

There are a number of ways of doing this, although basically each method has an identical aim in attempting to throw the weight of the crew (skipper too, in some cases) as far outboard as possible. Some dinghies merely require the crew to sit high on the gunwale and lean out when

Skill and co-ordination are required for trapeze work

the boat heels. Others have boards or similar arrangements to enable the crew to scramble right outboard of the boat. But the maximum righting effect is achieved by the *trapeze* which is a harness suspended from the top of the mast enabling the crew hand to swing himself right out to the full extent of his body.

Balancing is an art which comes almost entirely by practice. Furthermore, practice with one particular boat and skipper is important, for in addition to balancing, the skipper prevents the boat from capsizing by easing the main sheet and spilling wind. Thus the trapeze man must be able to anticipate when the mainsheet is eased, as throwing his weight too far out when there is insufficient breeze in the sail may result in a 'backwards' capsize.

When the pressure on the sails causes the boat to heel, the crew lean backwards. As the pressure and heel increase, so the weight of the crewmen's bodies is forced further and further out over the side of the boat. When maximum righting effect has been achieved, and the crew cannot swing out any further, the skipper must ease the main sheet to prevent the boat heeling any further.

He must be careful, however, to ease only sufficient sheet to spill the excess wind, or sudden loss of pressure will cause the boat to come upright suddenly and throw the crew hand into the water. Hence the need for close co-operation between skipper and crew when sailing in strong or squally breezes.

There are no hard and fast rules to apply to balancing. Methods differ according to the types of boats and individual preferences. Generally speaking a toe-strap should be located conveniently for the crew to obtain some grip on the boat when swinging in and out. When fastened into his harness a trapeze hand should always be in such a position that he just clears the gunwale when swinging out over the side. This puts him in a good position when he is stretched right out on tiptoe in a direct line off the deck of the boat.

To throw their weight even further outboard, some trapeze men lean back with their arms above their heads (see Fig. 32). This is a good stance, providing the forward leg is

FIG 32   **Trapeze position**

kept stiff, and makes for quick recovery if the wind drops
suddenly.

Quite often—particularly in boats with only two crew—
the trapeze hand is also the sheet hand and he must operate
the jib sheets as best he can from his precarious position.
The skipper, too, has much the same problem. Although
not swung out in a trapeze, he will be leaning right out
against the heel, but must still continue to control tiller
and possibly mainsheet also. For this reason an extension,
which is known under a variety of names, including 'hiking
stick', is added to most small boats' tillers.

The art of balancing a dinghy is a large part of the art
of being able to sail a dinghy. The maintenance of maximum
drive, by keeping the sheets on as much as possible and
spilling as little wind as possible, is the secret of sending
the boat speeding across the water. This can only be achieved
by correct and quick adjustment of balance.

Chapter 8 **Rule of the Road**

When a large number of yachts or sailing dinghies are racing in close proximity, a special set of rules is necessary to prevent collision between them. At other times, however, there is usually room to observe the likelihood of a collision and the approach of another vessel on collision course in time

Port tack (foreground) must give way to Starboard tack

to take avoiding action. Thus there are very few rules of the road for general use, and they are quite simple.

For yachts other than those taking part in an official race, the following rules apply.

1.   When two yachts are approaching in such a way that a collision may take place:

(i)   If they are on opposite tacks the vessel on the port tack gives way to the vessel on the starboard tack.

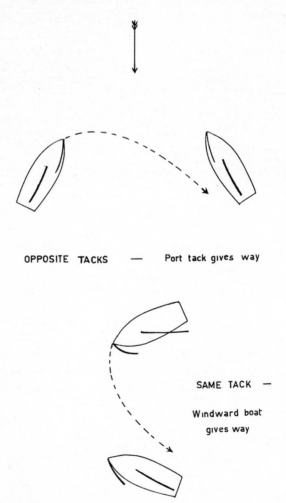

OPPOSITE TACKS   —   Port tack gives way

SAME TACK —

Windward boat gives way

FIG 33 **Giving way**

Windward boat (large yacht) must give way

   (ii)   If they are on the same tack the vessel which is to windward gives way to the other.

2.   Power gives way to sail.

3.   Any overtaking vessel keeps clear of the vessel being overtaken.

4.   A sailing vessel gives way to a vessel under oars.

5.   A sailing vessel gives way to any *hampered* vessel (i.e., a vessel manoeuvring under difficulty . . . dredge, tugs, etc.).

6.   Although not a rule in the legal sense, it is a generally accepted courtesy for yachts that are not engaged in racing to keep clear of all yachts in a race.

N.B.   There are often special local rules concerning large power vessels such as ocean going ships and ferries which nullify some rules. Such rules apply only within a certain harbour or zone, and when entering an unfamiliar port the yachtsman should be sure he is familiar with any such rules.

Chapter 9 **Heavy Weather**

Someone once said that sailing a yacht through a storm
was like standing upside down in a cold shower tearing
up ten pound notes. How true this is. There can be no other
condition onshore or at sea which is more uncomfortable and
more heart-breaking than sailing through rough weather.

Heavy weather usually results from fresh winds over 17
knots (Force 5). But the real sailing problems arise with
violent gusts (brief increases of wind speed), squalls (more
prolonged increases of wind speed) and gales (sustained wind
speeds of Force 8 or over). Although weather forecasts may
give ample warning of troubles ahead, local conditions vary
and can bring unexpected changes of fortune.

Normally, a yachtsman with any sense (and any stomach)
will put into port to ride out a storm. But during an ocean
race, or on a long-distance journey, it is often not possible
to shelter, and the storm has to be ridden out.

Seasickness is something which affects almost every
yachtsman, and there would be no more than a handful
in any yachting centre who could *honestly* say the motion
of a heavy sea does not upset them. Those few are the lucky
ones. The majority suffer from this, most miserable of all
maladies. Without doubt *mal de mer* is a great handicap
in stormy conditions. And in some parts of the world,
especially the southern hemisphere, big swells with very
low winds can be a cause of sickness. Whatever the
conditions sickness may be avoided by staying on deck or
by making sure you lie down when below.

While there are tablets which claim to alleviate seasickness
and, no doubt, some of them work, the violence of a yacht
in a seaway for the most part is something that not even
modern medicine can subdue, and the violent churning of

84

a stomach in that yacht is something which must be grinned at and borne.

These are but a few good reasons for riding out a storm in the quiet shelter of a harbour or bay. However, if it *is* necessary to be at sea, then the routine of preparing for, and riding out a blow, should be studied, as the latitude for mistakes is small under such conditions.

The first procedure, as the strength of the wind increases, is to reduce sail, and this is where the hard work comes onto the shoulders of the crew. The jib must be changed for a smaller one, and the mainsail reefed to balance with the smaller jib and the strengthening wind. If the yacht is only cruising then this is a relatively simple operation. The jib can be dropped and the boat sailed on the main while another jib is bent on. If racing, however, such a procedure would result in the slowing of the boat for too long a period and a faster method of changing headsail must be employed.

Some racing yachts have two forestays, enabling a new jib to be bent on and hoisted while continuing to use the

Heavy weather

FIG 34 **Storm sails**

old. Where this is not the case, however, the following procedure enables a new jib to be bent on with minimum delay.

1. Take the new jib forward and lash it to the pulpit. Unclip the lower two hanks on the present jib.

2. By means of a spare tackle, fasten the tack to the deck, and clip on to the forestay all the hanks of the new jib in the space created by releasing two hanks on the old.

3. Pass the sheets of the new jib aft and through the sheeting blocks. All is now ready for the changeover.

4. Quickly lower the present jib, unclipping the hanks as it comes down. Switch the peak shackle from the old to the new jib and immediately hoist the new jib.

5. When the new jib is set and drawing, the old jib can be unshackled and taken aft to be re-stowed.

Reefing the Mainsail

The old method of reefing with reefing points is so outdated and involved, and leaves the sail in such an unusable bundle it is not worth mentioning here. If roller reefing is not provided, it is better to reduce sail by dropping one or other of the sails and continuing with this reduced rig.

With roller reefing, however, the sail can be quickly and effectively reduced to any required stage. The procedure is as follows:

1.   Slack away the main halyard slightly. Ease main sheets.

2.   Insert the roller reefing handle into its socket and commence turning, ensuring that as the sail rolls on to the boom, the luffrope (or tape) winds evenly.

3.   When the slack of the halyard has been taken up, ease it more, and continue winding the reefing gear.

4.   Continue until the correct amount of sail has been reefed. On main sheet and continue sailing.

Changing the headsail and reefing the main are sufficient for a moderate blow. However, should the wind increase in intensity, the sails will have to be taken off altogether and replaced by storm gear. This comprises a very small jib and equally small, *loose-footed* mainsail. Each yacht will have its own system of setting up storm gear, and this should be checked over before leaving port if there is any likelihood of its being needed.

Once set, storm gear is controlled in the same way as a normal suit of sails.

Heaving To

It may happen that the skipper decides not to try to sail out the storm. In open ocean, or anywhere where there are no immediate hazards or a nearby coastline, the yacht may be hove to. This allows her to ride out the storm with the maximum of comfort and safety, a factor appreciated greatly by an exhausted crew.

There are two methods of heaving to. One, mentioned in Chapter 4, involves the backing of the sails against one another. However, it is more likely in a storm, that the sails will have to be dropped altogether; then the boat is hove to by means of a *sea anchor*.

The sea anchor, which should be provided on every yacht putting to sea, consists of a canvas bag, or *drogue*, tapered from about three feet diameter at the mouth to about eighteen inches at the tail, and with a rope bridle that will keep it consistently filled with water when dragged through the waves.

The sea anchor is tossed over the bow (never the stern unless the yacht has a canoe stern) and paid out until it

is about *two wave lengths* away. If it is allowed to drift
only one wave length away, it will not be fully effective
as the wave carrying the boat and the wave containing the
sea anchor will move together, reducing drag to almost
nothing.

FIG 35 **Riding to sea anchor**

By paying out plenty of line, the sea anchor also lies
deeper in the water, giving an even better 'bite' when the
pressure comes on to it. As a wave pushes the boat's head
off the weight comes on the line and the drag of the canvas
bag full of water pulls her back into the wave, thus holding
her head to wind and sea, the most comfortable position
in which to heave to. (See Fig. 35.)

Riding it Out

There are a number of schools of thought on how best
a yacht should ride out a storm. Some advocate lying ahull
(without any sea anchor or other means of preventing drift)
and some a sea anchor or rope over the stern and run with
the seas. Doubtless some of these may have merit, but a
yacht is designed to go into the sea bow first, and whether
under sail or whether hove to, I cannot but feel that this
is the most comfortable and safest position for her to ride.

Heaving to is only practical when clear of any coastline
or other danger, as the boat, when hove to, makes a certain
amount of drift to leeward. A yacht should never be close
inshore in heavy weather and should head out to sea as
soon as the storm develops if shelter is not available. Far
more vessels have been lost trying to make for shelter on
a coastline than have foundered in the open sea during
a storm.

Safety

Whatever sailing decisions the skipper makes when a storm comes up it is very important for him to ensure that the safety of his crew, himself, and his craft is given every consideration.

Of course, everyone on board must be wearing a life jacket and all deck hands must put on safety harnesses or lifelines with strong fittings and lines. Personal safety measures are just as important in the cockpit as on the foredeck for a violent change of wind direction or a wave breaking over the deck can easily knock somebody overboard.

Cockpit lockers must be closed and watertight and if there is an engine hatch it must be screwed down tightly. All gear must be carefully secured (don't forget the spinnaker pole!) with extra lashing as seems necessary. If the boat is carrying a dinghy or raft ensure that it is given extra lashing too.

Double-check that small items of equipment like winch-handles, balers and paddles are secure.

Finally, every crew member must have a clear idea of his responsibilities in heavy weather conditions. The noise of heavy seas and the deafening effect of wind and driving rain can make it difficult for the skipper to communicate and he may not have time to explain details of procedure to someone who doesn't know what to do. For this reason everyone who intends to sail where heavy weather may be encountered is well advised to read one of the excellent books on the subject and to discuss the problems of seamanship and safety with his colleagues.

Chapter 10 **Emergency**

It is a fact that, although most emergencies arise as a result
of carelessness or negligence, there is always the odd case
that is just a matter of bad luck. Whatever the cause,
the essential thing about an emergency on board a boat
is the ability of skipper and crew to cope. And to be able
to cope with an emergency means to have foreknowledge
of what to do in the emergency, and to be prepared when
it strikes.

Generally speaking, sailboats are much safer than power
boats. They do not have to depend on mechanical means
for propulsion, which eliminates possibilities of mechanical
breakdowns. They derive their power from the wind and,
therefore, cannot run out of fuel, or if so, only temporarily.

It happens to everyone!

And they are so designed that they are more 'sea-kindly'; that is, they can ride out heavier seas with safety and reasonable comfort. Most important of all, of course, a yacht with a weighted keel cannot capsize.

In fact, a yacht is just about the safest form of waterborne transport. Even allowing for it to lose its mast and rigging, the boat will float upright in a safe position until emergency repairs can be effected. If it is rolled over by a freak wave, it must bob up again because of its weighted keel. It can never stay upside down. Although most people who sail for the first time in strong winds get the feeling that there could not be any craft *less* safe, this is only a superficial impression, as they are not oriented to the heel of the yacht.

Even so mishaps do occur, and in this chapter a mention of some of the more likely accidents may make the reader more prepared in the unfortunate event of such an accident happening on board his vessel.

Capsize

Although virtually impossible in a well-found yacht, capsizing is the most likely thing to happen to a small sailing dinghy.

When a yacht is hit by a strong gust of wind, she heels well over, but cannot possibly capsize, for the further she heels, the less the direct pressure on the sails until, if she theoretically reaches the horizontal position, the wind simply passes right over her. The pendulum effect of the keel brings her back to the upright as soon as the pressure on the sails is relieved.

In practice a vessel rarely heels as far as this because the pressure on the sails slackens and the pendulum effect of the keel begins as soon as she starts to heel out of the vertical. In fact, a happy balance of forces is usually achieved when the yacht is heeling in the 30 to 40 degree zone. This is an ideal situation for sailing, because the sails are taking maximum power without spilling too much wind over the top, and the keel has not been lifted out of the water, resulting in the boat drifting sideways.

Should a sudden squall knock her further over she will

return as soon as the squall eases. If it does not ease then she is over-canvassed and sail must be reduced. Here can be seen the importance of the right sail for the right weight of breeze.

A sailing dinghy, however, whilst having the same arrangement as a larger yacht above the waterline, has no counterbalancing keel. Thus if a squall strikes and she heels too far, although the pressure on the sails will slacken as she heels further and further, there is no pendulum effect of the keel to bring her back to the vertical, and unless some other means of righting her is found, she will flop over on her side.

As mentioned in the chapter on balancing (chapter 7), the crew use their own bodies as counterbalance weights. However, a crew needs to be very nimble to counter every suddent gust, and often they are caught off guard and the boat capsizes.

FIG 36 **Using the centreboard as a lever to right a capsized dinghy**

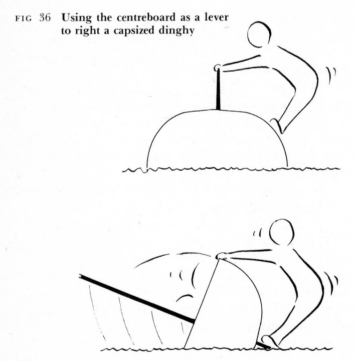

There is no great problem in righting a small boat. To bring her upright the sheets must be freed, and one or more crewmen must climb onto the centreboard and use his weight to bring her back upright.

There are many small boats fitted with self-draining cockpits, and the minute they are brought to the upright position, the water inside drains out. Where this is not the case one crew hand must clamber on board and bale out with a bucket or similar baler while the rest of the crew holds the boat steady, head to wind. Once the boat has been righted the centreboard should be lifted as it helps to fill the centreboard casing and prevent an inrush of water whilst baling out.

Once the level of the water has been taken down a reasonable amount, the rest of the crew can clamber aboard and the boat sailed to a nearby beach, to be drained out completely. If there is a self-baler fitted, she will complete the draining process herself as she gets under way.

When sailing in a dinghy a few important pointers should be remembered, against the chance of a capsize:

1.   *Tie in the baler.* Nothing is more frustrating (and potentially dangerous) than righting the boat only to find the baler has sunk.

2.   *Ensure the boat has sufficient buoyancy.* She must float, completely waterlogged, with both gunwales above the water. If not, it will be impossible to bale her out.

3.   *Fasten the sheets and halyards on deck or on the mast* so that they are attainable when the boat is lying on the sails before righting.

4.   *Wear lifejackets. Even if you swim* you never know just how long you may be in the water.

5.   *Never leave the boat.* This last is a most important rule. Distances are hard to judge when in the water, as also are currents. As long as you stay with the boat (and she floats) you have support. The author came close to drowning through leaving the boat to swim after a wallet that floated off. The drift of the boat and a strong current made it impossible to regain the boat, and a mile-long swim in choppy seas resulted.

Dismasting

This usually occurs in strong winds and is due to faulty or incorrect rigging. It does not create a very great emergency as a rule, since the boat is not usually damaged by a falling mast, and even if it is, it can be patched up temporarily. On board a large yacht it is merely a question of cutting away the rigging, ensuring that there are no ropes or stays hanging over the side, and returning to shore under power, or with the assistance of a tow.

Because the mast in a smaller craft is stepped on deck or in some accessible place, it can often be re-rigged and set up again. If the mast itself is broken, of course, this cannot be done, and it is then a question of gathering up the bits and starting the long paddle home.

Grounding

Since dinghies sail on and off a beach as a matter of course, grounding is not foreign to them.

A most unpleasant occurrence when grounding a dinghy unexpectedly is to snap off the centreboard, or punch a hole in the bottom on some submerged object. In this case, since the boat must be in shallow water, she can be hauled ashore and repairs made.

When a deep keel yacht grounds, it is a different proposition. Considerable strain can be put on a boat, particularly if there is a big sea running. Also, as the tide falls, the yacht will fall over on her side unless shored up, and will fill with water the next time the tide comes in. Although the best method of getting a grounded yacht off varies according to conditions, the following will be of use.

1. As soon as she has grounded, release the sheets. All hands should then be moved to one side of the boat to heel her. If she is heeled sufficiently, the keel will be lifted off and she may be moved off by power or, if it is a weather shore, by sail. (See Fig. 37.)

2. If she will not move even when crew are perched right out on the end of the boom in an attempt to heel her over, she will have to be lightened by throwing ashore all equipment and, if possible, internal ballast.

94

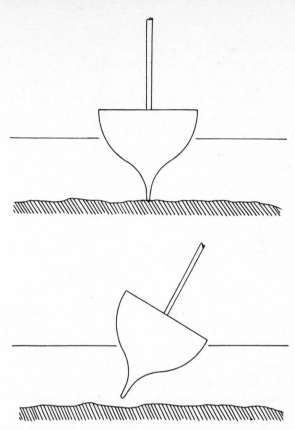

FIG 37 **Inducing heel to free a grounded
yacht**

3.   If she will still not move, it will be a job for a tug,
and since the boat will have to remain aground she must
be shored up against the falling tide. As the tide falls, rigid
props made from the spinnaker pole or from other lengths
of available timber must be driven into the sea floor and
propped against the boat's side so that they support her
beneath the rubbing strake.

Fire

This is undoubtedly the worst hazard encountered on board
a boat. Since it almost never occurs in small dinghies, we
shall concentrate on action to be taken with fire on board
a yacht.

FIG 38 **Basic 'fire triangle'**

Obviously the best precaution is to have adequate, *tested* extinguishers on board. It is not sufficient to store an extinguisher down below somewhere and forget about it. Most modern extinguishers depend on chemical reaction and the chemicals inside them can deteriorate with age. The extinguisher itself will be marked with a safety date, and these should be checked regularly. It is too late when facing a fire out at sea to discover that the extinguisher should have been refilled two years earlier.

However, there are occasions when an extinguisher is not handy, or when they have been used up, and other means must be used. Naturally there is a large fire extinguisher all around and beneath the boat, but water can be used only on certain fires, and it is not enough to say that with a bucket on board and the sea outside you can put out a hundred fires. Most fires on board come from oil, petrol or fat, and none of these can be extinguished with water. Quite the reverse, in fact; pouring water on an oil or fat fire will actually spread it and make it worse.

When water cannot be used, the fire must be smothered. Buckets of sand, if available; if not, blankets, sails, or any other enveloping material which will stifle the fire.

Remember always the basic 'Fire Triangle'. Fire can exist only if three things are present: Combustible material, oxygen and heat. Take away any one of these things and the fire cannot develop. This is the factor on which all firefighting techniques are developed.

First Aid

The recovery of a man overboard has been dealt with in another chapter. Once he is on board, he must be treated. Two major factors contribute towards fatalities due to falling overboard—drowning and immersion, or heat loss. It is important, therefore, to know the various forms of resuscitation as well as treatment for heat loss and shock. A first-aid book should be carried on board a yacht of any size, covering most normal injuries, and in fact a complete first aid cabinet is a good idea, as yachting is a tough sport at times and takes its toll of minor injuries and accidents.

It is not possible to carry such an outfit in a dinghy, of course, and in any case, the boat is usually within easy reach of the shore in the case of an accident. However, it is worth remembering that drowning alone is not the cause of fatalities in the water. Be prepared for heat loss when sailing in colder waters. Thick sweaters—the ideal protection, a rubber skin-diving suit—are advisable when the temperature of the water is sufficient to give trouble. Most definitely a life jacket must be worn, whether one can swim or not.

Calling for Assistance

Once again this section is concerned mainly with the larger yachts which, when well out to sea, are out of easy reach of assistance. A small boat in difficulties in a bay will be quickly spotted, and the very nature of the difficulty will bring assistance. But at sea, well offshore, there are fewer boats about, and it may not be apparent to either boats or shore stations that a vessel is in difficulty unless she uses one of the prescribed forms of distress signal.

Many yachts carry radio telephone equipment which enables them to keep in contact with shore stations. If a boat is in serious difficulties it can seek help by using the international distress frequency, which is 2182 kHz (kiloherz), on which a twenty-four hour monitor is kept. The stations observe three-minute silence periods at regular intervals for the express purpose of listening for distress calls.

over the air, one of the following signals may be used to attract attention. They are international signals and are set down here in the order considered most suitable for small vessels:

1. *A bucket of burning oil rags.* This is the most useful and most efficient method for small craft. By day it gives off thick smoke; by night, flames. It will immediately attract attention, even that of boat skippers who may not know this is a recognised distress signal.

2. *Hand flares.* These are specially made flares which can be held in the hand and waved. They emit both smoke and flame.

3. *Rockets.* Again these are specially made distress signals which burst into red stars and are recognised distress signals in any part of the world.

4. *Heliograph.* This is a mirror or a piece of shiny metal which can be used only in daytime to reflect the sun's rays in the direction of a shore station or a nearby boat.

5. *Distress Signals.* The International Code flags for signalling "I am in distress and require immediate assistance" are the two letters NC hoisted N above C (N is a chequered blue and white flag, C is horizontally-striped blue white red white blue from the top).

6. *Dye Marker.* This spreads through the water, leaving a bright stain visible from the air.

Other, improvised, distress signals or means of attracting attention may be used, but it is wiser to know and use the accepted signals. How often has someone in trouble waved frantically at another boat, only to have their wave gaily returned.

Finally, remember that prevention is better than cure. A safe vessel is one that rarely encounters difficulties, and such a vessel is safe only if both skipper and crew pay thorough attention to the needs of safety, both when preparing the vessel for sea and also when working aboard her. As the old windjammer sailors advised their new chums, when on board a ship no matter how big or how small:

One hand for yourself, and one for your ship.'
In that order.

Chapter 11 Ropes and Cordage

The arrival of synthetic materials hailed a revolution in the world of sailing. Dacron, terylene and nylon became names synonymous with ease of handling, lightness and efficiency. Nowadays almost every craft afloat is partially or wholly fitted with synthetic gear, and the 'tough' old days of hard ropes, blistered hands and hours of maintenance work are gone for ever.

So many are the advantages of the new materials over the old that they are almost too numerous to include in a chapter such as this. But they are rot-free, impervious to salt water, light, extremely tough, durable, long lasting and almost free of maintenance. Their light weight enables smaller and lighter accessories to be used, reducing the weight of blocks and fittings which were so cumbersome on older vessels. Their strength and working life are phenomenal; most yachts using synthetic running gear find it lasts five or six times longer than cotton or manila.

In addition they may be stowed away wet without fear of mould or rot, and in many cases do away with the need for splicing at loose ends. A lighted match can be used to melt and fuse the loose ends of a synthetic rope together, eliminating the need for splicing or whipping.

Thus terylene, nylon and dacron ropes are to be found throughout the yachting world. Together with sails of similar material, they offer a combination that is almost unbeatable. So the days of canvas sails, with the inherent need for washing and drying after use, are also numbered. Although manila, hemp and sisal ropes still find considerable use on the water, particularly when larger sizes are required, they too are feeling the competition from synthetics as far as smaller craft are concerned.

Synthetic ropes are usually made up in one of two ways; *laid* rope, which is the normal twisted strand method used to make fibre ropes, and *braided* rope, which is a form of plaiting, resulting in a softer, more pliable rope. Both are equally useful, the only real advantage being in the softer, more usuable form of braided rope.

Synthetic cordages are made up in much the same way, most being of the braided variety. With the need for whipping diminished by the newer types of ropes, cordage in synthetic material is usually confined to light material for sewing or lashing.

Knots and Splices

As mentioned earlier, the advent of synthetic ropes has lessened the needs for splicing. It is virtually impossible to splice braided rope at all, and laid synthetic can in many cases replace a normal splice with lashing or fusing. However, the old tradition of sailors' knots has survived the impact of the new materials, and the need for a good knot is actually even more important on synthetic rope than on the fibre ropes, due to the slipper surfaces of new synthetics.

The secret of a sailor's knot is that it will hold under any conditions, wet or dry, slack or taut, but will never jam. If it is correctly tied, the knot can be released quickly and surely by reversing the direction of the pressure. It is obvious how useful such a knot can be under such conditions as freeing a jammed rope or releasing the gear of a capsized dinghy.

Most knots are designed to do a specific job, and a good sailor will take the trouble to learn as many as he can to cover all eventualities. However, in this chapter a few of the essential ones are shown and no sailor, no matter how inexperienced, should put out in a boat without first learning these knots.

In the following descriptions the term *end* means the handling end of the rope. The term *standing part* applies to the main section of the rope.

FIG 39 **Reef knot**

THE REEF KNOT

Used to join together two pieces of rope of almost equal
circumference. Take one end in each hand. Holding the
left rope firmly, place the right hand rope over the left
then around and under it. Turn the loose end of the left
rope back on itself and place the right hand rope again
over it and then under it. The result is the reef knot in
which the standing part and the handling end of the rope
come out of the knot together. If they do not come out
together the knot is called a Granny knot and will jam.
To release the reef knot, grasp both standing part and
end of the left rope and push it into the knot. The knot
will fall apart.

FIG 40 **Single sheet bend**

FIG 41 **Double sheet bend**

THE SINGLE- AND DOUBLE-SHEET BENDS

The single sheet bend is used for joining together two ropes of *unequal size*. Take the larger rope in the left hand and form a loop towards the body. Do not cross the end over the standing part. From underneath the loop push the right hand end up through the loop, around to the right and behind the loop, back across the face of the loop and under its own standing part.

The double sheet bend is also used for joining together two ropes of *unequal size*. First make the single sheet bend as described previously, continue to pass the end of the right hand rope once more around the back of the loop (in the larger rope) across the face of the loop and under its own standing part. In short, twice around the loop of the larger rope instead of once.

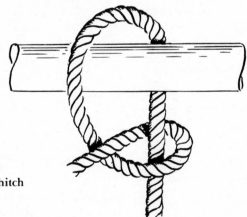

FIG 42 **Half hitch**

Used to tie a single end of rope to any fixture such as a ring, rail, etc. The end of the rope is taken around the fixture, then crossed over its standing part from right to left, and finally pushed through the loop thus formed. This hitch is only a temporary hitch and may easily work free; the pressure has only to be relieved from the standing part in order to release it.

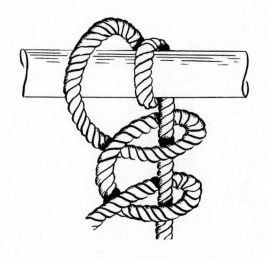

FIG 43 **Round turn and two half-hitches**

ROUND TURN AND TWO HALF-HITCHES

For securing a single end of rope to a fixture. This hitch is more secure than the single half hitch and can be used for tying up a boat painter, or making any fairly permanent attachment as it is difficult for it to work loose.

Place the end of the rope around the fixture, then take it round once again. Form a half hitch after the second loop, then repeat with another half hitch immediately below the first.

FIG 44 **Figure-of-eight knot**

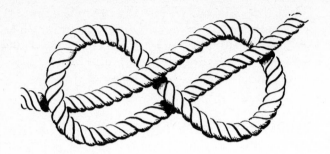

FIGURE OF EIGHT KNOT

Used as a stopper to prevent the end of a rope slipping through a block. Take the standing part of the rope in the left hand with the end towards the body. With the right hand take the end back over the standing part crossing from right to left. Pass the end round behind the standing part, back over itself and through the loop. To release, push the end back into the knot.

FIG 45 **Bowline**

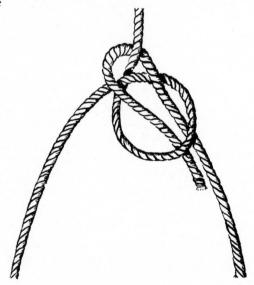

THE BOWLINE

Used for making a loop in a rope, usually for mooring ropes. Take the standing part in the left hand, with the end towards the body, allowing sufficient rope to make a loop of suitable size. Twist the standing part into a small loop at the left hand with the main part of the rope underneath. Take the end in the right hand and pass it up through the small loop, around the standing part from right to left and back down through the small loop. Hold the end and loop and pull the standing part tight. To release push the standing part into the knot.

FIG 46 **Clove hitch**

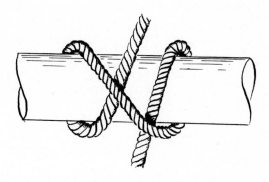

THE CLOVE HITCH

Used for a multitude of purposes where rope has to be attached to any fixed object. Pass the end around the object and back on the right hand side of the standing part. Pass it around again, but this time crossing to left over the first loop. In bringing the end back from the second loop bring it inside the loop to the right of the standing part. To release, ease the pressure on either end of the rope.

Glossary

Aback: (Caught aback). Wind on the wrond side of the sails.
Abeam: 90 degrees from dead ahead on either side.
Aft: At the rear; nearest the stern.
Ahead: In front.
Anti-fouling: Special paint used on underwater section of hull.
Anti-cyclone: High pressure system.
Astern: Behind.

Back: Reverse a sail; get the wind on the wrong side.
Backstay: Stay running from masthead to stern.
Ballast: Weight used to stabilize a boat; exterior ballast (on keel) or interior ballast (in bilges).
Bear away: Alter course away from wind.
Belay: Make fast.
Bight: Loop in a rope
Bilges: Curve of hull where keel is attached.
Bobstay: Wire stay beneath bowsprit.
Bollard: Post for attaching mooring ropes, etc.
Bonnet: Additional fair weather sail.
Boom vang: Small tackle attached to under side of boom.
Boot-topping: Line between anti-fouling and topsides.
Bow: Forward section of boat.
Bowsprit: Spar sticking out ahead of boat for securing forestay.
Broaching: Dangerous condition caused by vessel slewing sideways in following seas.
Broad-reaching: Sailing with wind just abaft the beam.
Bumkin: Spar sticking out astern for securing backstay.

Centreboard (or plate): Movable fin keel in sailing dinghies.
Chain plates: Plates securing rigging to hull.

Cleat: Metal fitting for securing lines.

Clew: (of sail). After corner.

Close-hauled: Sailing as close to the wind as possible.

Coach-house: Cabin roof.

Coaming: Side surrounding cockpit or hatch.

Come up: To round up towards the wind.

Companion way: Entrance to cabin.

Cross trees: Cross spars on mast to spread rigging.

Crutch: Fitting to hold boom when mainsail is not set.

Cyclone: Depression; low pressure system.

Dead-eye: Eye fitting used for sheets.

Dead square: Sailing with wind dead astern; boom right out.

Deck-head: Ceiling.

Depression: Low pressure system.

Diamond shrouds: Mast rigging which does not reach deck line.

Dog house: Raised section of cabin.

Down tiller: Tiller pushed to leeward.

Downhaul: Rope used to tie down spinnaker guy.

Draft: Depth of water from waterline to bottom of keel.

Drift: Direction of wind.

Ease sheets: Order to slack out sails.

Ebb: Outgoing tide.

Fairleads: Fitting for ropes or marking chain.

Fisherman: Sail set by schooners between the masts.

Flood: Incoming tide.

Foot: (of sail) Lower edge.

Forward: Ahead.

Foremast: Forward mast in schooner.

Gaff: Boom at top of sail (gaff rig).

Genoa: Large jib.

Ghoster: Large light weather jib, usually quadrilateral.

Golliwobbler: Very large light weather jib, similar to ghoster.

Gooseneck: Fitting attaching boom to mast.

Goosewing: Sailing with jib and main on opposite sides (wind astern).

Gudgeon: Circular fitting attaching rudder to boat.
Gunwale: Top planking of small boats.
Guy: Rope used to control spinnaker pole.
Gybe: Change tack with wind astern.

Halyard: Rope used to hoist sail.
Handing: Taking off the sail.
Hanks: Clips attaching jib to forestay.
Heave to: Holding vessel in stationary position head to wind.
Helm: Tiller.
Highfield lever: Lever used for tightening rigging.
Hiking stick: Extension to tiller.
Horse: A rail or track around which main sheet tackle can move.

In irons: Head to wind, sails not drawing, vessel stationary.
In stays: Another term for in irons.

Jam cleat: Gripping mechanism used on sheets of small boats.
Jib: Head sail.

Kicker: Down haul.

Laid deck: Timber deck comprising small planks.
Leach: (of sail) Trailing edge.
Lee: Side away from wind (lee shore).
Lee-Oh: Order given when going about.
Leeway: Sideways drift caused by wind pressure.
Luff: (of sail) Leading edge.
Luffing: Sailing too close to wind.
Luff rope: (or luff tape) Reinforcement on leading edge of sail.

Mainsail: Sail set to main mast and boom.
Mast cap (mast head): Fitting at top of mast.
Mizzen: Rear mast of ketch or yawl.
Mizzen staysail: Sail set between masts on ketch or yawl.

Peak: (of sail) Top corner.
Pintles: Rudder fittings set into gudgeons.
Port: Left-hand side facing forward.

Pulpit: Rail set around bow or stern for safety.

Quarter: After section of boat.

Ratlines: Cross rigging on main shrouds.
Reaching: Sailing with wind abeam.
Ready about: Warning prior to going about.
Ready to gybe: warning priot to gybing.
Reefing: Reducing sail.
Rubbing strake: Protective wooden band below gunwale.
Runners: After rigging stays.

Samson post: (see bollard).
Scuppers: Gutters around outer edge of deck.
Set: Current.
Sheer: Curve shape of hull.
Sheets: Ropes controlling sails.
Sheeting blocks: Pulleys through which sheets are led.
Shrouds: Rigging on side of mast.
Shy reach: Sailing with wind just ahead of beam.
Spinnaker: Full cut sail used for reaching or running.
Spreader: (see cross trees).
Squall: Sudden gust of wind.
Stanchion: Supports for life rails.
Starboard: Right-hand side facing forward.
Stays: Fore and aft mast rigging.
Staysail: Head sail set on stay.
Stem: Bow.
Stern: Rear end.
Stern gland: Opening through which propellor passes.

Tabernacle: Fitting on deck into which mast is stepped.
Tack: (of sail) Forward corner.
Tack: Side on which wind is blowing (starboard tack);
    working into wind (tacking).
Telltale: Ribbon or twine in rigging to indicate wind
    direction.
Toe rail: Raised outer edge of deck.
Topping lift: Rope or wire holding boom in place.
Topsides: Exterior of hull between waterline and deck.
Transom: Flat stern.

Triatic stay: Stay between two masts.
Truck: Top of mast.
Turnbuckles (or bottlescrews): **For tightening rigging.**

Up tiller: Tiller pulled to windward.

Warp: Anchor line.
Weather: Windward side (weather shore).
Weather helm: Amount of rudder adjustment needed to cope
    with strength of wind.
Whisker pole: Small pole used on small boats for holding
    out jib.
Winch: Drum fitting used for tightening sheets and halyards.
Windlass: Winch used for heaving up anchor.
Windward: Side from which wind is blowing.

Yankee: Large jib flown with cutter rig.
Yawing: Cork-screwing action of boat in following sea.